TEARING DOWN
# STRONGHOLDS

# TEARING DOWN
# STRONGHOLDS

*and Defending the Truth*

R. C. SPROUL JR.

P&R PUBLISHING
P.O.BOX 817 • PHILLIPSBURG • NEW JERSEY 08865-0817

Scripture quotations in the introduction and chapter 2 are from the HOLY BIBLE, NEW INTERNATIONAL VERSION®. NIV®. Copyright © 1973, 1978, 1984 by International Bible Society. Used by permission of Zondervan Publishing House. All rights reserved.

Except in the introduction and chapter 2, Scripture quotations are from The Holy Bible, New King James Version. Copyright © 1979, 1980, 1982, Thomas Nelson, Inc.

*Page design by Tobias Design*
*Typesetting by Michelle Feaster*

Printed in the United States of America

**Library of Congress Cataloging-in-Publication Data**

Sproul, R. C. (Robert Craig), 1965–
    Tearing down strongholds : and defending the truth /
R.C. Sproul, Jr.
        p.   cm.
    Includes index.
    ISBN-10: 0-87552-702-7 (pbk.)
    ISBN-13: 978-0-87552-702-4 (pbk.)
    1. Apologetics. I. Title.

BT1103 S67 2002
239—dc21
                                                2001059105

*To Rev. Martin Murphy,*
*defender of the faith*

# CONTENTS

# PREFACE

Awkward circumstances are all the more so when you must share the awkwardness. It's bad enough, for instance, to lock yourself in a bathroom. It's worse when you have to ask your wife, or your children, or the neighbor, or the paramedics to get you out.

Writing this book put me in an awkward situation. My desire was to help laypeople come to a basic understanding of the foolishness of unbelieving epistemologies (theories on how we know what we know), and to help them reach a sound epistemology. With the first goal I presume that many Reformed scholars would cheer me on. The awkward part is the second goal, wherein I am advancing a view that is well outside the current mainstream of the Reformed world. And I've had the audacity to ask *the* Reformed publishing house to help me.

My prayer is that as avid Reformed apologists read this, they will see my heart's desire, and there would be rapprochement in the war within our walls. I would love to see presuppositional and classical apologists getting along like the brothers they are. (And if you, reader, don't know those terms, don't worry. This book is mostly for you.) I believe we agree on more than we know. I believe we both need to listen more carefully to each other. I believe we are both fighting on the side of the angels.

If that can't happen, I pray at least this—that any fire-breathing folks on the other side of this intramural battle will not blame my friends at P&R for being kind enough to get me out of the locked bathroom. They did not ask me to pray for this. In fact, I don't know if this little request will make it past the editors there. But please do not let their grace to me cause you to be anything but gracious to them.

I would especially like to thank Allan Fisher and Thom Notaro for all their labors. They not only unlocked the door, but did so without making me look like a fool. Thanks are also due to my dear wife, Denise, and finally to my students at the Highlands Academy and the Highlands Study Center, who helped sharpen these ideas through God's great gift of conversation. I also owe a debt of gratitude to Dr. Andrew Hoffecker, who first showed me the folly of fools. And deepest thanks are due to my two greatest teachers, my earthly father, and my spiritual grandfather, Dr. John Gerstner.

# INTRODUCTION

Chess is a tricky game. I don't play very well, for I suffer from two deadly weaknesses. First, I am impatient. I'm in too much of a hurry to think through the implications of a given move. Any opponent who has the capacity to think a few moves ahead has me in his crosshairs. If I do manage a victory, it's usually because my opponent gave me too much credit and was thinking several wise moves ahead, only to be flummoxed by my silly moves.

My second weakness is that I am too aggressive. My game of chess resembles Pickett's Charge. I send my pawns to the slaughter, all in a vain attempt to get at that queen. Chess is a game of strategy, not a game of will. Wanting it badly enough does you no good.

The key to good chess is to understand its nature. It's not by accident that chess pieces have the names they have. Chess is ultimately the game of war writ small. We have infantry in the pawns, cavalry in the knights, castles in the rooks. And the goal of the game is to topple the king. And if you can break through the defenses and land on enemy soil, well then, you can have all the queens you like and destroy with all the aplomb of barbarians.

War operates under the same basic principles. While we would like to think that the key issue is the morale of the troops, that wanting the victory brings the victory, the two key issues are really the strength of one's arsenal and the wisdom of the strategy employed. There is a delicate balance to be found. Mass your troops into a wedge, and you will find yourself outflanked and surrounded. Spread them too thin, and your lines will be pierced. The wise commander keeps in mind three key issues. First, he must repel the attacks of the enemy. Second, he must defeat the enemy in a given battle. And third, he must always seek and serve his ultimate objective. If winning a battle causes him to lose the war, he might as well have stayed at home.

Apologetics is warfare writ large. Here the stakes are not mere bragging rights at a chess table. Neither are the stakes a comparatively petty issue like who will rule a nation. Chess is just a game, and nations come and go. Truth, and the souls who encounter Truth, both last forever. That the stakes are so high, however, should not drive us to draw our swords and charge ahead thoughtlessly. The wise man fights with his wits.

One of the oft overlooked tactics in warfare is the use of propaganda. Perhaps the most fruitful volley in a given war is the one that persuades one's enemies that there really isn't any war going on at all. If the enemy is persuaded that peace has been declared, then the war is already won.

That has been the strategy practiced of late by the leader of the forces of darkness, Satan. He has created a culture in which tolerance is the greatest virtue, in which the freedom of religion recognized by the state is confused with freedom from God. In creating and selling us the idea that we shouldn't discuss politics or religion in polite company, the devil has put us to sleep. There is a war going on, and it began back at Eden.

The devil fired the first shot, and it came from a mighty howitzer. His barrage consisted of this question: "Has God said . . . ?" That sneak attack by the devil seemed to secure him a victory, at least in that battle. But we would be wise to remember that every victory of the devil is actually a defeat for the devil. Our King, because he is absolutely sovereign, ultimately moves all the pieces on the board, and so every move for him is a victory. Our King responded to the devil's attack with a solemn declaration of war:

> So the LORD God said to the serpent, "Because you have done this, Cursed are you above all the livestock and all the wild animals! You will crawl on your belly and you will eat dust all the days of your life. And I will put enmity between you and the woman, and between your offspring and hers; he will crush your head, and you will strike his heel." (Gen. 3:14–15)

This battle, the struggle between the seed of the serpent and the seed of the woman, is the context for all of our lives. The end is certain, for God Most High declared to the promised Son, "Sit at my right hand until I make your enemies a footstool for your feet" (Ps. 110:1). The battle is not waged principally with swords and fighter planes.

> For though we live in the world, we do not wage war as the world does. The weapons we fight with are not the weapons of the world. On the contrary, they have divine power to demolish strongholds. We demolish arguments and every pretension that sets itself up against the knowledge of God, and we take captive every thought to make it obedient to Christ. (2 Cor. 10:3–5)

The devil would have us believe that because we do not use the weapons of this world, we are not at war.

But notice Paul's language here. These are not polite and delicate words. We are not going to the seed of the serpent and suggesting politely that their view of things might be slightly mistaken. We don't plead, nor do we market. Rather, we are demolishing these arguments, recognizing that they are pretensions set against the knowledge of God. The warfare of winning souls is not fought against innocent noncombatants who just need to be led in the right way, but against those who have pledged allegiance to pretenders to Christ's throne. To be sure, our prayer is that these children of the serpent will become heirs of the King. To be sure, such were we before we were conquered by Christ and his church. To be sure, we are to love our enemies. But we must love them enough to utterly destroy the lies they believe, so that they might be born again.

But here again we would be wise to recognize the condition of our enemies. While we are called to tear down strongholds, the lost are not kept from the kingdom merely by wrong thinking. The devil, after all, is a Calvinist. That is, he believes that God is sovereign, and that Jesus lived a perfect life for God's elect and received in their stead the sanctions of the covenant, the wrath of the Father. He understands the gospel much better than we do, so that if we could get him to speak the truth, he would be a great teacher. He knows the truth and knows that the lies he has set up in place of the truth are lies. But he hates the truth. The winning of souls is so much more than presenting compelling arguments for the truth of the gospel, but it is not less. Scripture clearly teaches that the Spirit gives life. The lost are not merely wrong, but dead. If the Spirit did not give life, all my apologetical endeavors would be nothing but speaking to the dead.

Winning apologetic arguments is not the same thing as winning souls. The Spirit may work through apologetics to win the lost, but that is ultimately the work of the Spirit. If we speak the truth, and the Spirit gives ears to hear, our only response is to sing, "Not unto us, O Lord, is the glory of the victory due."

The goal of apologetics is to destroy falsehood and to proclaim and defend the truth. Truth is the hill that must be taken. And the purpose for taking the hill is the same as the purpose for doing all things: to bring glory to God. Although the Spirit is not constrained by our ignorance or our sin, we cannot expect that he will be at work if we are practicing apologetics for our own glory, to look wise in the eyes of the world.

That threefold goal of apologetics—destroying falsehood, proclaiming truth, and defending truth—might be seen as the three fronts of our war. The first, destroying falsehood, I call "positive negative apologetics." That paradoxical term illustrates what we are trying to accomplish. It is positive because we are on the offensive. In this battle, we are trying to dislodge the enemy from his position. It is negative because we are not seeking to prove anything, but rather are seeking to disprove something. Our goal here is not to show the truth of the Christian faith, but to show that the faith of the enemy is necessarily false.

In waging this type of war, reconnaissance is critical. We are doing the lost no favor if we attack positions they have left behind. We can assault the hill for days on end, but if there is no one there, we've just been wasting our ammunition. Neither should we attack a hill our enemy has never inhabited. Attacking ideas no one holds is akin to bombing empty fields. We ought to be able to describe and understand the other man's position well enough that we can define and explain it to his satisfaction. Straw men are easy targets, but they don't make for very satisfying victories.

As we shall see, this part of the job is perhaps the easiest. Scripture tells us, "The fool says in his heart, 'There is no God'" (Ps. 14:1). On this particular battlefield, we are engaged in a battle of wits with half-armed men. On the other hand, when the ideas of fools come to dominate a culture, the culture begins to make foolishness look like wisdom. This is why we are enjoined, "Do not conform any longer to the pattern of this world, but be transformed by the renewing of your mind" (Rom. 12:2).

This reminds us of some collateral benefits of this particular battle, even when the Spirit does not regenerate lost souls. When we are given new hearts by the Spirit of God, we still struggle in our thinking. That is, we remain under the influence of the world around us. Sound apologetics may not set the lost free, but it may bring the found closer to the image of Christ in their thinking and ultimately in their doing. The more apologetics shows the thinking of this world to be the folly that it is, the less we on this side of the battlefield will be under the influence of the world.

The second of our three kinds of apologetics can serve the same purpose. We need to remember what I so often forget in chess. While we are attacking, we are also being attacked. This might be called "negative negative apologetics." It is negative first because we are acting defensively, responding to the attacks from outside. It is also negative because we are not yet developing our positive case. Though positive support for our position is implied, in this aspect of the battle, we are emphasizing that attacks on our position are not true.

Here too we must listen carefully to the words of our opponents. When we answer objections that they are not making, we are defending a flank that is not being attacked. That not only depletes our resources, but can also make us look foolish. We must listen to their objections and treat them as honest objections. We do this even though their objections aren't honest. As we have noted, Scripture teaches that the unbelief of our enemies is a moral problem, not an intellectual one. But we cannot expect anyone to listen to us if we will not even entertain the possibility that our thinking or arguments or some of our assumptions may be flawed.

When I was in college, I had a good friend who was studying to be an engineer. We often talked about the things we were studying. I wanted to argue Einstein with him; he wanted to argue theology with me. For the most part, not surprisingly, he did better with Einstein, and I with theology. One day, after a sound thrashing, my friend said, "You just win because you're better at arguing than I am." I'm sure my response surprised him: "If that's really the way you feel, Hans, then I guess we will have no more discussions of theology. If you will not concede, no matter what, then why am I spending my time on this?" I argued in the hope of changing his mind. If I argued well, I expected him to change his mind.

We must not have a mind-set like my friend Hans. We should not use any kind of special pleading or defend our position with bogus arguments. While it is true that the unbeliever hates the truth of the Christian faith because it condemns him, a seemingly good point that he makes is not adequately answered by saying, "You just say that because you hate God."

Neither are we to reply, "Well, that may not be true for you, but it is true for me." Our humility, our posture of accepting that we are fallible, is not the same thing as adopting the position of relativism. As our opponent begins to attack our position, we respond this way: "I believe that my position is in fact the objective reality of the universe. However, it is possible that my argument or understanding is flawed. My commitment is to the truth. If you can show me where I am wrong, I will concede." That is a fair, honest, and humble position for us to take. Then we are truly doing the work of apologetics as we defend the faith against the attacks of those who deny it.

But suppose we successfully repel every conceivable attack against the faith. Suppose our opponent lies exhausted at our feet, having run through every argument he could find in his "Devil's Field Guide to Attacking the Christian Faith." Each objection was masterfully answered. We still have not done our job. We have, using our negative positive apologetics, shown that his view holds no water. We have, through negative negative apologetics, shown that our view is not vulnerable to attack. But we haven't made any progress in establishing what the truth actually is. We haven't done the work of what I call "positive positive apologetics."

Positive positive apologetics is called such because we are developing a case, and making that case for what we believe to be true, not merely against what we believe to be false. And here is where the real work is. This labor is so difficult that some of our allies in the Christian camp will argue that it cannot be done. Some believe that the best way to make the case for the Christian faith is simply to meet the other guy on the battlefield, destroy him, and, if we're still standing after enough battles, maybe people will give us some respect. If people see that the Christian faith has not been defeated by objections, then maybe they will think there's something to it.

The trouble with this view is that one never knows whom one will meet on the battlefield of the future. If I defeat a thousand five-year-olds on the chessboard, that doesn't mean I'm invincible. Perhaps the next person to sit across from me will be Bobby Fischer. I can't make the case that I'm the greatest player of all time simply by beating all challengers, for one never knows what challenger may be around the corner. The Christian faith is not simply better than all the others; it is true. And so it must be shown to be so.

There's another variation on that same theme. Some would argue that since the Christian faith explains reality better than any other available worldview, it must be true. But the same problem remains. Maybe a new faith will come along that gives an equally plausible explanation of all things, or perhaps an even better one. Sound positive positive apologetics makes the case that the Christian faith is not only the most likely explanation of reality, but also the only one that can be true.

I write from the perspective that the Christian faith is true, and that it alone is true. To lay that before you is not to confess my bias. It is true that I was raised in a Christian home, that I grew up in the church. That makes my faith neither unassailable nor necessarily false. It is likewise true that the Christian faith is the center of my life, my reason for being. Without it, I know not into what depths of despair I would sink. But wanting to believe the Christian faith makes it neither true nor false. I believe the Christian faith to be objectively true, independent of my belief in it, because I believe it has been shown to be objectively true. And so I claim that if I have any bias, it is a bias in favor of truth and opposed to falsehood. But to call that a bias is to distort the meaning of the word beyond all recognition.

My hope is to persuade others and to provide some tools to help others persuade others. My goal is not only to tear down the strongholds of the devil, and not only to re- pel the assaults of the very gates of hell, but to show that the foundation upon which our faith stands is firm. I set out to do this prayerfully, for the God of all truth is also the God of all power. And the God of all power has told us truth's name: Jesus.

## PART ONE

# THE END OF THE DINOSAURS

## CHAPTER ONE

# THE DARKNESS OF THE ENLIGHTENMENT

The Reformers were good with slogans. Although they were prolific writers, they also had the capacity to boil down the essence of their convictions into short, pithy phrases. One could spend a lifetime unpacking the powerful messages contained in the *solas* of the Reformation. The first *sola* was *sola Scriptura,* meaning "Scripture alone." It opposed the Roman Catholic view that church tradition is equally binding on the consciences of men. This was the "formal cause" of the Reformation. The issue of justification, the "material cause," came down to *sola fides,* "faith alone." It affirmed that we are justified by the imputation of Christ's righteousness alone through faith alone, contrary to Rome's claim that we must become righteous by our cooperating with the infusion of grace. *Solo Christo, sola gratia*—all of them were and are bound together in the greatest of the *solas, soli Deo gloria,* "to God alone (be) the glory."

But to put the Reformation in its historical context, the Reformers had another phrase, *post tenebras lux,* "after darkness, light." For many years, the church had wandered in the darkness of Rome's Babylonian captivity. But this darkness came to an end when God, in his grace, once more shed the light of the gospel upon his church.

Words have meaning, and words have power. When we are engaged in the battle for truth, oftentimes the first ground we must seize is that of good words. For example, political races are often won today by conservative candidates who campaign for "family values." Who could be against families? Some candidates who are more liberal, however, have sought to win back the word with the slogan seen on bumper stickers, "Hate is not a family value." With one short phrase, they have sought to regain "family" and pin "hate" on their political opponents.

"Light" and "dark" are the same kind of words as "family" and "hate." Although Scripture says that sinners hate the light and love the darkness, not too many of us advertise that fact. In the battle over words, we all want to portray ourselves in the light and the other guy in the dark. Thus, the Reformers of the sixteenth century cast Rome in the dark and themselves in the light.

But not long after that, the tables were turned. The eighteenth century was a time not so much of reformation as of revolution. Many philosophers and other thinkers sought to eliminate not only church tradition as a source of knowledge, but revelation itself. No longer would men be blinded by the darkness of the Word of God; now they were coming of age and seeking to understand the world armed with human reason alone. This movement was called "the Enlightenment."

The Enlightenment embraced a wide range of thinkers and ideas. Its influence was felt not only in the world of ideas, but also in the world of politics. Then, as now, ideas had consequences. On this side of the ocean, the Enlightenment had a powerful influence on some of our founding fathers. Ben Franklin, Thomas Paine, and Thomas Jefferson all drank deep from the Enlightenment well. Many have argued that the American Revolution was made possible by a strategic alliance between those committed to Enlightenment ideals and those committed to the authority of Scripture, between the deists and the Christians. This coalition gave us "nature and nature's God" as the transcendent source of the rights of men.

In France there was no such coalition. There the Enlightenment was essentially undiluted, and the result was the French Revolution and the Reign of Terror. There Enlightenment thinkers allied themselves with Madame Guillotine. The result was not freedom, but a greater tyranny than was felt under Louis XVI.

With respect to theology, the Enlightenment thinkers were by and large deistic. In their view, there was a God who had created the universe, but he was both largely unknowable and largely absent from the world. He was the clock-maker God, who wound up the universe and went out for a walk, never to return. For them, the God hypothesis was a matter of convenience. An explanation was needed for the existence and order of the universe. Having provided such, God was excused from the scene, lest he start demanding things of us. It took Darwin's theory of evolution, a seemingly plausible explanation for our existence without a creator, to allow God to die in the minds of many "enlightened" men.

With respect to anthropology, the study of man, the Enlightenment was rather enthusiastic. Man was deemed to be fundamentally good. The Fall was a myth of revelation. Rousseau argued that man was a noble savage. The existence of evil could be explained culturally. Good children learn bad habits from the corrupt influences of society and church. (Rousseau never adequately explained how noble savages created corrupt institutions in the first place.) Put man back into his natural state, and he would do just fine.

This denial of the Fall had a profound influence on Enlightenment epistemology. Epistemology has to do with how we know things; it is the study of the nature and grounds of knowledge. Without the Fall, man's mental faculties were deemed to be in fine working order. Man had the capacity, on his own, to discover all the truth he needed. Revelation was just so much useless dogma. Reason would lead the way to paradise.

This brings us to Enlightenment eschatology, or the study of last things. Here the view was essentially evolutionary. Every day in every way, man was getting better and better. What was needed to deal with human problems was a fundamental reordering or dismantling of society. If we could just get the gum of revelation and church dogma out of our minds and the minds of our children, then the engines of human progress would run smoothly and we'd get somewhere. The Enlightenment was perfectionistic. It taught that with the right sociological techniques, the right educational methods, the right exercise of political power, and the right harnessing of machines, we can have heaven on earth. We have the minds and the will to do it, and so we can.

One can already see, I hope, the storm clouds on the horizon. Perhaps the Enlightenment wasn't such a bright idea after all. This worldview combines two ingredients that are extremely volatile when mixed. It is one thing to believe that one has the capacity to create heaven on earth. It is altogether different to hold that view and at the same time deny that there is a transcendent and revealed law that binds our conscience. What present cost could be too high if we are convinced that our work will usher in utopia? It wasn't so much rage that fueled the massacre in France as it was an unswerving conviction that excising the cancer of wrong-thinking people would lead to eternal life.

The excesses of the French Revolution certainly damaged the confidence of some in Enlightenment optimism. But with the scientific method as the model for knowing truth, we know that one failure just means we need to tinker with the experiment a little and try again. Perhaps what was needed was a more gradual approach, or perhaps a more drastic one. Therein lies another danger in the Enlightenment ideal. While modern men might agree that we are on the road to paradise, without a celestial or transcendent road map, there are bound to be some serious arguments about how to get there.

One of the most fundamental disagreements grew out

of the view that rationalism was a rather sterile way of knowing things. All the machinery of civilization, some said, was stifling. And from this dissatisfaction was born the romantic movement. The reason we keep getting lost on the yellow brick road is that we are already there. All we need to do is click our heels together three times and repeat "There's no place like home." The romantics found that the clockwork model of the universe was too mechanical. Rather than turning back to a transcendent revelation, however, they posited the idea that the world is more like a living organism. The romantics and the rationalists agreed that there was nothing over the rainbow, no transcendent source of knowledge, ethics, or purpose. They disagreed over whether those things were found in our head or in our heart.

The siblings continued to bicker through most of the nineteenth century. Each took great pleasure in pointing out the faults of the other and in boasting of their own accomplishments. Thus, with every new invention—the cotton gin, the steamboat, the telegraph—we were treated to more cheers for rationalism and more assurances that paradise was just around the corner. Meanwhile, the romantics countered by pointing to some of the excesses of the Industrial Revolution. A walk through the working-class neighborhoods of New York, London, or Edinburgh might persuade one that paradise was yet a ways away. And while their own failures tended to be somewhat more personal (a visit to an opium den to see the great romantic poets might clue you in that all was not right with their worldview), so were their successes. A small painting or a book of verse wasn't the most compelling evidence that the romantic train was bound for Eden. But one shouldn't expect grand displays of progress for a worldview bound up in the heart of the individual.

As their battle for preeminence raged, the failures on both sides began to mount. The utopian communities that popped up across the American landscape proved to be failures. The romantic movement burned out, or rather was subsumed under the rationalist regime. Now the vision of an Enlightenment paradise was not being peddled by engineers, but by poets. That is, the rhetoric heated up, and the two movements combined in a series of moral crusades. Whether it was the Society to Prevent Cruelty to Animals, Dr. Graham's (the inventor of the Graham cracker) crusade to get us all to eat less processed food, the early temperance movement, or the assorted utopian communities that dotted the land in the late nineteenth century, what was needed was zeal.

After a host of failures, the crusaders turned to the issue of women's suffrage. Their cause was interrupted, however, when a bomb was dropped on the playground of the Enlightenment. All of Europe went to war. World War I was war like the world had never seen. It was the first war to engulf a continent, the first war to be fought with sophisticated and deadly weaponry on both sides. It was the first war to destroy not only battlefields, but cities. It seemed as though the dreams of the Enlightenment simply dissipated into the air with the deadly nerve gas.

But optimists and visionaries do not give up easily. If war was the great scourge of the human community, what was needed was a government sufficiently powerful, and sanctions sufficiently horrible, to make it no longer possible. So the victors of Europe finished the war with two monuments to the Enlightenment, the League of Nations and the draconian Treaty of Versailles. Germany, having been roundly defeated, was ordered to pay reparations beyond their ability and to decimate what remained of their war machine.

In the East, the Enlightenment vision of Karl Marx was finally given its opportunity to shine. The Bolsheviks seized power with all the tact and delicacy of their French revolutionary forbears. Here science would reign, and the outdated notions of a transcendent deity would be educated out of the minds of the people. What were needed, in the Soviet Union and around the world, were Enlightenment visionaries who would hold the reigns of power, control the economy, and train future leaders in Enlightenment theology. Now that the war to end all wars was behind us, we could get on with remaking Eden.

But the best laid plans of mice and men frequently come to naught. The government's manipulation of the economy in the United States created the glow of prosperity after the war. The moral crusaders managed at least to send the demon rum into hiding. And happy days were here again—until Black Friday. The paper wealth that the Federal Reserve had manipulated into existence fell into a black hole as the stock market collapsed. And the force of the economic gravity pulled down with it whatever real wealth had once existed. And the ripples went forth into Europe, spreading the depression there.

The trouble with the slow-moving process of making utopia is that the scientific method cannot tell us whether our failures result from the intervening Enlightenment schemes or what remains of the Christian culture. And so, with each successive blow, the people called out for more of the new and less of the old. Accordingly, Roosevelt gave us a New Deal and a new concept of freedom.

To the Christian mind, freedom in the political sphere was a negation. That is, the goal for those who loved freedom was a state whose role was limited to protecting life and property. It was upon this principle of limited government that the country was founded. But now, in the midst of economic hardship, Mr. Roosevelt promised freedom from fear and freedom from want. Big government would not be the threat to, but the source of, our new freedom. And thus the welfare state was born.

Meanwhile in Europe, it was becoming apparent that Germany wasn't dead yet. It was just wounded and very angry. The war machine was back up and running, and Germany went in search of new lands to conquer. The fascist movement mixed together the brutal efficiency of the Enlightenment with the ethical vacuum created by Nietzsche and rolled across Europe. The Enlightenment was coming apart at the seams, at least among the philosophers. The brute exercise of power for the sake of creating a new world was reduced to the brute exercise of power for the sake of the brute exercise of power. And the state became God.

Again, all of Europe, and most of the rest of the world, was at war. Japan masked its will to power with a more clear religion of the state, emperor worship. Ironically, this war was essentially decided not by who could exercise the greatest control over the citizens, nor even by who could build the biggest war machine, but rather by who could build the smallest war machine. That is, as the war went on, it became apparent that the nation that could harness the power in the atom would win.

The victory of the Allies, however, was a hollow victory. It was not so much the Axis powers that were destroyed by the Allies, but the Enlightenment dream. The experiment had failed. Two world wars, a worldwide depression, and the mushroom clouds over Hiroshima and Nagasaki had shown it to be a cruel and deadly farce. Now technology promised not to lead us into the promised land, but to destroy the land in which we lived. It is difficult to persuade the young that we've almost reached the promised land while they are huddled under their desks in a darkly comical drill to prepare for atomic attack.

Everyone admitted that our technology had outrun our wisdom. And perhaps nothing illustrated this more than the images of Germany that returned from the death camps. Here was a people holding onto a transcendent revelation of truth, of right and wrong, and they had been largely wiped out. The hollow shells of the cathedrals of Europe, the symbols of an older and better civilization, drove home the point. But of course the war wasn't over. The race for Berlin, as the war in Europe came to an end, reminded us that though we had defeated our enemy, we had done it with the help of an equally, if not more, brutal regime. As the Iron Curtain descended on Eastern Europe, we geared up for another struggle, the Cold War.

Our confidence was gone. By now the word was out that Stalin had failed to create his utopia, even as Chairman Mao imposed his vision upon China. So many experiments, so many failures. Perhaps the problem wasn't the assorted theories of how to build the utopia, but the idea of building one at all. Perhaps the failure wasn't in failing to find a nontranscendent source of truth and ethics, but in asserting the idea of truth and ethics. First we struggled through a war pitting fascism and emperor worship against Communism and the welfare state. After that was over, the battle raged between Communism and the welfare state. It seemed that too many nations were too sure that they knew what was good for us. A healthy dose of skepticism might have helped us keep our swords in our scabbards.

As we pursued détente, it may have seemed that Communism works for those in the East, and that the welfare state works for those in the West. We can both be right, can't we? But all this technology, all this technique, just seemed to get us into trouble. And so the Enlightenment experiment went into the ash heap of history. Or, to put it in slightly different terms, after God was banished, the assorted states that filled the vacuum failed to give the world a consistent and coherent vision, and instead went to war. And so, down with visions.

The French, you will remember, responded to their defeat in World War I by building the Maginot Line, a seemingly impenetrable defense along their border with Germany. But the Nazis responded by going around that defense, and attacking through Belgium. In the continuing battle of worldviews, the Christian church has too often made the mistake of the French. We have too often fought the current war by using the weapons of the previous war. Today, we are out hunting for modernist Enlightenment dinosaurs, while the world belongs to the bastard children of the modernists, the postmodernists. The battle is no longer over whether science or religion will give us truth, but over the very existence of truth.

It is true that there are yet some dinosaurs left. But they are few and far between. It takes an ocean of credulity to yet hold out hope for the coming paradise in the face of our twentieth-century experience. But while we may rejoice that one foe is fast on its way to extinction, that history has proved the scientists and social engineers wrong, we find that a new and far more dangerous and crafty enemy has taken over. In fact, it was the very failure of Enlightenment truth to deliver the goods, or the very defeat of our old foe, that has so empowered the new foe. To the postmodern mind, the truth claims of the Christian faith sound just like some new angle on the old Enlightenment. We look like dinosaurs, not because we affirm an old truth, but because we affirm truth at all.

The first battle, then, is the battle for truth. This is why J. D. Hunter, in his book *Culture Wars*, argues that the battle lines are now drawn between the orthodox and the progressives. The orthodox he defines as those who uphold transcendent truth, transcendent ethics, even while arguing among themselves about the source. The progressives, in his view, deny both, affirming the truth that there is no truth, and the ethic that says it is wrong to speak of right and wrong.

But here again we would do well to learn the lessons of our history. We must be careful of the nature of the alliances we make with those who share our conviction that genuine truth and right exist. After all, if there is genuine truth, it cannot be both the Scriptures and the Quran. If there is objective right and wrong, it cannot come both from Scripture alone and from Scripture plus tradition. In the battle for truth, we cannot settle for anything other than genuine truth.

There is another battle, perhaps an even more important one, that we must wage. It is not enough to be king of the philosophical hill. It is not enough for our champions to defeat their champions. For the battle is not just fought in the culture, but in our own hearts and minds. A worldview may be shown to be downright silly, and yet affect our own thinking. If we fail to tear down strongholds, let us at least take our own thoughts captive in subjection to Christ, the captain of our salvation and the captain of the Lord's armies.

## CHAPTER TWO

# NEGATIVELY POSITIVIST

The French were neither the first nor the last nation to pin their hopes for military success on what they perceived to be an impenetrable shield. The people of Jericho rested easy at night behind their great wall, believing it could never come tumbling down. They were dead wrong. God is stronger than any wall ever constructed.

One of the troubles with walled cities, as Jerusalem discovered when Rome conquered her in A.D. 70, is that they are susceptible to siege warfare. If nothing comes into the city, pretty soon folks get hungry and thirsty. One king figured he had that problem licked. King Belshazzar had a mighty empire. He likewise had a mighty wall. But he also had water, for under his wall ran a river. Belshazzar was so confident that his city could not be taken that he ordered a feast in the midst of a siege. And, as we remember, he was so certain of his own power that he defied God Most High by ordering that the holy implements from God's temple be used during this banquet. But soon the handwriting was on the wall, quite literally.

The banquet first turned ugly when a hand was seen writing on the wall. "This is the inscription that was written: MENE, MENE, TEKEL, PARSIN" (Dan. 5:25). And Daniel was called in to interpret.

> "This is what these words mean: *Mene:* God has numbered the days of your reign and brought it to an end. *Tekel:* You have been weighed on the scales and found wanting. *Peres:* Your kingdom is divided and given to the Medes and Persians." Then at Belshazzar's command, Daniel was clothed in purple, a gold chain was placed around his neck, and he was proclaimed the third highest ruler in the kingdom. That very night Belshazzar, king of the Babylonians, was slain, and Darius the Mede took over the kingdom, at the age of sixty-two. (Dan. 5:26–31)

Darius knew exactly what to do when walls tower over you. You go under them. He dammed the river upstream from the city, and as Belshazzar celebrated his invincibility, the soldiers of Darius marched into the city on the dry riverbed. And thus a kingdom fell.

In the warfare that is apologetics, the foundation is always epistemology. If one can establish the parameters of truth such that one cannot lose, the battle is over. If I could get my opponents to accept an epistemology that said, "Whatever R. C. Sproul Jr. says is true," then my victory would be total. Thankfully, that isn't possible. But the

citadels of all false worldviews are built upon the foundation of false epistemologies. We can argue with the conclusions of these false worldviews. We can send cannon shot
into their walls. We may even penetrate at a place or two.
But to tear down the stronghold, we must get to the bottom
of it. We must destroy the foundation.

As laborious as this might seem, if the Christian
worldview is correct, it really won't be so difficult. If the
Bible is true, then only fools say in their heart that there is
no God. And fools should fear us, not we them.

The fundamental weapon of our warfare against the
foundations, ironically, is the foundations themselves. The
weakness is always found when we test the epistemology
against itself. If it fails this test, it shows itself to be necessarily false. And if the foundation does not hold, down
comes the whole wall.

We looked at the fruit of the Enlightenment. We argued that things have gone too badly over the last few hundred years for Enlightenment optimism to have any
credibility. But remember that with each social calamity,
there were those who yet held out hope that the problem
wasn't the principles of the Enlightenment, but their application in that particular instance. And we mentioned that
there yet remain some holdouts even now in our postmodern
age. The good news is that we don't need to wait for more
calamities to chip away at what remains of Enlightenment
optimism. We can demonstrate that the epistemological
foundation of the Enlightenment is necessarily false. And we
do it, as we have indicated, by testing it against itself.

Remember also that the Enlightenment is a reactionary movement. That is, it is defined more by what it is against than by what it is for. It is against any idea of supernatural revelation as a source of truth, and for any source of truth found in men. But one view of the source of truth came to dominate. The Enlightenment first became optimistic in an era of rapid growth in knowledge, and in the application of that knowledge to technology. We managed to sail across the ocean. We harnessed first the power of flowing water to create the factory. We then improved upon our use of water, creating the steam engine. More and more goods were made for more and more people. There came in rapid succession the railroad, the cotton gin, the mechanical loom, the telegraph, and the lightbulb.

Perhaps nothing better illustrates the principle of applying the scientific method than Edison's faithful work on the lightbulb. We begin by observing nature. We guess how it works. We construct a test to see if our hypothesis is correct, if it accounts for all the results. We then seek to apply our hypothesis to produce power. Edison knew that if you supplied a certain amount of electricity in a certain way, it would excite certain things to give off energy in the form of light. The problem was to find the right substance to let the light shine. Edison, we're told, tried hundreds of substances until he hit on the tungsten that we still use today.

While change can bring social upheaval, as the Industrial Revolution did, the consensus was surely that things were getting better. In the West, the fear of widespread starvation became a thing of the past. We advanced so rapidly in our capacity to produce goods and services that many came to fear that we had outstripped our capacity to consume what we produce. Some argued that our problem was not scarcity, but overabundance. That is a comparatively good problem to have. And what got us there was the application of the scientific method.

As so often happens, we as a culture seek to take what works in one realm and apply it across the board. If the scientific method could solve our economic problems, many thought, perhaps it could solve all of our problems. The application of the scientific method to human problems created what came to be known as the social sciences. A pioneer in the social sciences was the French philosopher August Comte.

Comte was born in 1798, and he is credited with being the father of sociology, a term he coined in 1830. In it, he tried to apply the scientific method to social issues. He also developed a hybrid of epistemology and eschatology to explain the growth of man's thinking. He divided history into three parts. The first stage he called the theological. Man, in this stage, sought to understand and manage his existence by thinking in theological terms. That is, change was attributed to the actions of a god or gods. Man was defined in relation to a god or gods.

As man progressed, he left behind this theological framework and developed a metaphysical or philosophical understanding. Revelation was left behind, and man had to think his way through the issues he faced. This was, to Comte, a change for the better, but still not the apex of man's thinking.

The third and final stage he called positivism, or the scientific age. In this stage, answers are found, not in revelation or in the confines of one's mind, but empirically—that is, through the senses. Comte believed that man was beginning to enter this final stage and would remain in it, happily, forever. However, Comte, like so many others, lost some of his optimism when the empirical data still showed great social upheaval.

Such upheavals, however, did not destroy the root of the problem. Positivism reached its peak with a group of thinkers known as the Vienna Circle. They came under the sway of such modern philosophers as Ludwig Wittgenstein and Bertrand Russell (who wrote the classic agnostic work, *Why I Am Not a Christian*). Positivism grew into logical positivism. It declared that only those ideas which can be empirically verified (that is, verified through the senses) have any meaning.

It was here that the battle lines between science and Christianity were clearly drawn. But it is helpful to realize that it has not always been this way. The scientific method is driven by induction. We induct when we make generalizations after observing a set of particulars. We deduct when we reason from the general to the specific. For instance, if I were to ask a thousand men who claimed to be bachelors if they were unmarried, and they all said yes, I might reason by induction that all bachelors are unmarried men. However, if I knew that, by definition, a bachelor is an unmarried man, I would not have to ask any particular bachelor about his married state. I would know he is unmarried by deduction.

Induction can serve a purpose. Many of the earliest scientists were deeply committed to the Christian faith.

Their goal was to "think God's thoughts after him." God made a promise to Noah after the Flood that he would operate his creation in an orderly fashion, that night would follow day, and seasons would follow a discernible pattern. Given God's promise of regularity in the natural world, induction is a valuable tool for exercising godly dominion over the creation. Without it, it is gratuitous.

Ask the unbelieving scientist why he believes that the sun will rise in the morning, and he will likely reply, "Because it has risen every morning of recorded history." He may get more technical and speak of the earth spinning on its axis. Then we must ask why he believes the earth will continue to spin on its axis. Sooner or later he will reveal his fundamental faith that things tend to stay the same, that the future will be like the past, unless acted upon by an outside agent. But there is still no reason to believe that. All the inductive evidence in the world cannot establish the validity of induction. That is, unless we assume that things stay the same, the fact that they have stayed the same is no evidence that they will continue to stay the same.

The point here is not merely to get on even ground, to thumb our noses at the scientists and hurl at them the accusation they hurl at us, that they are resting on faith. It is not enough, when dealing with the logical positivist, to point out that he rests upon faith, just as you do. That works out to a tie, which isn't how we tear down strongholds. It does reveal, however, that any success that a false worldview has, comes from premises taken from a biblical worldview. Scientists have given us all that they have given us only because they expect uniformity from nature, an expectation that logical positivists—indeed, anyone who denies God's existence—have no reason to affirm. They assume design, but deny the Designer. It is not science that has made progress possible, but the sustaining hand of God. Remove that hand from your thinking and you cannot even tell the difference between progress and regress. Under the sun, even the most advanced technology is still nothing but striving after the wind.

When we elevate induction, and, by extension, empirical observation, to the pinnacle of our thinking, or rather use it as the foundation, we have another, more serious problem. It, like all other false epistemologies, fails its own test. Here is the quick, easy, and deadly refutation of logical positivism: If only those statements which can be empirically verified have meaning, we can rule out one statement's meaning right off the bat, namely, the statement that only those statements which can be empirically verified have meaning. The foundational principle of logical positivism is ruled out of bounds by the foundational principle of logical positivism. Epistemological claims are by their very nature abstract, and therefore not verifiable by the senses. I've seen, tasted, touched, heard, and smelled an awful lot of things in my life, but never an epistemological principle. The bastion of logical positivism, then, is self-referentially absurd. That's not the kind of reference you want.

The logical positivist, when teaching logical positivism, is actually speaking gibberish. One might as well adopt an epistemology that begins with, "Everything I say is false." If it is true, then it is false.

It can't be that easy, can it? It can. And it is. Remember that the sad truth is that most of us get our basic ideas of truth without giving them much thought. We embrace epistemologies for a number of reasons, not necessarily because they make sense. In a culture dominated by technology, it is easy for those who are unaccustomed to thinking in philosophical terms to embrace an epistemology that would be shown to be absurd with only a little thought, because they have given it no thought. Technology presents us with a double whammy. First, since science has done so many wonders for us, a "scientific" epistemology seems appropriate. Second, the profusion of technology has taught us to believe that only experts really know what's happening. I certainly don't understand how the computer I'm writing on works. When I have a problem, I call an expert and don't berate myself for my ignorance. And so, if the scientific experts say that this is how we know things, who are we to argue?

That, of course, doesn't explain how a Russell or a Wittgenstein could embrace a theory that is so patently silly. These men were geniuses. Perhaps they could not see this obvious problem because they were already so committed to the principle of induction. The goal in the scientific realm is to come up with a theory that explains all the data. Copernicus watched the stars dancing in the sky and couldn't explain it with a stationary earth. But if we assumed that the sun was at the center, and that the earth rotated around it, all of a sudden the dance made sense. Or at least most of it did. It took another scientist, frustrated with the remaining few anomalies (that is, bits of data that don't quite fit the theory), to suggest that if we understood the orbits as ellipses rather than circles, the data made more sense. If the scientific method can seemingly harness the power of the world, if we're having so much success with this method, let's make it the king of the methods. And if our theory of knowledge is an anomaly to itself, then that's just something we'll conveniently ignore.

But anomalies have a way of sticking around. The longer they stick around, the more imposing and obvious they seem to become. While those who thought up the idea might be rather attached to it and tend to overlook the warts, eventually others do begin to notice them and start looking elsewhere for an epistemology. And so the dinosaurs begin to die off slowly. That is not to say, however, that they are gone. There still exist priests of the religion of logical positivism, and most of them wear lab coats for a robe. It still influences our culture to a degree. Every time a space shuttle rises through the sky, or a new gadget is unveiled, we pay homage to our modernist fathers.

I don't know if it actually happened, but the story is told of the first Russian to be sent into space. Upon his return, he noted that he had looked out through the vast expanse of space and had not seen God. That idea still resonates in our culture. If you cannot test it with the senses, then it must not be real. And with this comes the weight of the experts. We won't believe anything until we read a report from some prestigious research council at some university. If we cannot have empirical proof, we at least want assurances from the priests of positivism. I've had many conversations with modernists who insist that they will not believe in God until they see him with their own eyes. (Rest assured that they will do both, one way or another.) But I've had even more conversations with people who insist that science has proved that there is no God. Who proved it? "They" did. Well, not only haven't "they" done so, but there is no "they."

It is not only belief in God, or even the positivist principle, that is outside the realm of the senses. Perhaps it was because the principle excludes not only a God who will judge, but also a love that will give joy, that so many romantics reacted against it, whether those romantics were Lord Byron or the dancing hippies at Woodstock. Although this is not definitive evidence against positivism (that is, the truth of something does not depend upon whether we like its implications), it certainly does tend to create a dull and joyless world. It takes the sublimity of a waterfall and turns it into so many water molecules being pulled down by gravity. It takes a mother's love for her child and turns it into so many chemical and electrical processes. It makes a cyber-world out of the real world. It does not, and cannot, explain love, courage, virtue, tenderness, or purpose.

Perhaps the loss of purpose is the most emotionally devastating fruit of positivism. It fails to give direction even to the science that it seeks to champion. It seems sensible enough to say that it is good to know why water cascades down Victoria Falls, but that cannot be demonstrated empirically. Positivists cannot prove that truth should be sought for truth's sake, but that is what they assume. To say that building better widgets is a good thing is to make another claim that is not empirically verifiable. Truth for prosperity's sake is also impossible in their system. Even to say that we should seek to persuade the world of the wisdom of logical positivism is not an empirically verifiable claim. The harder they work to persuade us of their claim, the more they prove that they themselves don't really believe it. Why bother to make the case, when the case precludes having a reason to make the case?

How does one determine whether it is better to create bombs capable of destroying the world or to find a cure for cancer, if one's only tools are things that can be empirically verified? What test tube answers that question? Did the Russian cosmonaut find out why it is better to go into space than not to go, while looking outside his space capsule? Here again, unbelievers are living off God's capital. When they seek to better our lives, they sometimes borrow our understanding of what better is. At other times their vision of what is better horrifies us. But they at least borrow the idea that some things are better than others. Better is something our eyes cannot discover. Though all of our decisions are ultimately determined by our values, those values are invisible.

Positivism has born its fruit. It created the gray and listless world of the Soviet Empire, an empire that could be propped up only so long by the stick of the secret police and the carrot of vodka. It also created the cold and sterile world of the "planned" neighborhood, whose many circuses distract us from the emptiness of our lives. The walls that positivism built not only are ugly, but cannot stand. Their foundation is sand. And it created a host of children who worked a little harder to explain the anomalies that are as plain as day. These children also tried to erect walls, but on the same unstable foundation. We will look at some of them in subsequent chapters.

## CHAPTER THREE

# UNNATURALLY NATURALIST

What is happening as you read this? I don't mean outside your window, but rather inside your head. You and I are having a conversation. But as I punch the keys on the keyboard, I don't know who you are, where you are, or even why you are reading. As I write, I'm guessing what you might be thinking as you read, trying to hold up your end of the conversation. And unless you are my wife, or my mom or dad, or a close friend, you probably know precious little about me. I could even be dead by the time this gets to you. We're having a conversation over time, over space. I am, in a manner of speaking, throwing out words.

Inside my head, I'm having another conversation, this one with myself. What do I say next? Is this going to be clear? Am I saying what I want to say, and am I saying it in an interesting way? And that internal conversation has worked its way out of my little brain, out through my fingertips, into this little box, past a vigilant editor, over to a printer, into paper and ink, and eventually into your hands. But it doesn't stop there. From the page, the words leap through your eyes into your brain, where you are quietly thinking. It's pretty amazing when you think about it, that our thinking works itself out in doing, which affects our thinking, which affects our doing.

There is an interchange going on between the world we see (light, ink, paper, the shape of these letters) and the hidden world of the mind. But there are those who would deny that distinction. They would argue that all that exists are matter and energy, which, Einstein showed us, are really the same thing.

The logical positivists have gotten into our brains. Seeing that we are human, that we seem to think, to make decisions, they have sought to find a way to explain all this in quantifiable terms. They have, through the work of men like Francis Crick and James Watson, reduced mind down to brain. They have not only denied the reality of what we might call the supernatural realm, but have denied that there is anything real that is not in some sense physical. Our nature is reduced to the sum total of our genetic alphabet. The thinking we do is nothing but a series of electrochemical reactions going on in the gray matter between our ears. And love is nothing more than the dance of the pheromones.

Watson and Crick, you will remember, were the scientists responsible for our understanding of DNA, for discovering the double helix. But, as so often happens, these brilliant men stepped outside their sphere, or rather, tried to shrink the world to fit into it. This notion is plausible because it is built on some truths. There are electrochemical reactions going on in our brains. Brain waves are measurable. We have them, and rocks do not. And though it is well outside my area of expertise, I'm sure that information is passed through our genes. My mother's father was bald, and I soon will be. And I expect my daughter Darby will raise up sons who will go bald, too. There is even a connection between genetics and our emotions. I'm not particularly happy about going bald.

As the Human Genome Project continues in its work of mapping the entire structure of human DNA, we are likely to hear more and more about which genes have what influence on our lives. Some suggest that a propensity for alcoholism is genetic; others say that various sexual perversions have their root in genetics. The difficulty will be to distinguish between genuine science and guesswork, between wisdom and foolishness.

Our tendency, as humans seeking to understand what it means to be human, has nearly always been toward reductionism. We find wisdom in parts, and seek to apply it to the whole. As we find that psychotropic drugs influence the way we feel, we then jump to the conclusion that our feelings are nothing more than chemical reactions. As we find that our hair color, or lack of hair, is a function of genetics, we then argue that all that we are is a function of genetics. And then we jump further and argue that because our feelings are merely chemical reactions, or our actions are grounded in genetic determinism, our feelings and actions need no justification. If indeed all that we are is reducible to chemicals, then how can we be held responsible for any of our thoughts, words, or deeds?

However, we are not reducible to chemical reactions. Our being consists of far more than our genetic makeup. And when people seek to persuade us otherwise, their efforts demonstrate that even they do not believe their own thesis. Just as I am writing this book to persuade you of the folly of their view, so they are also writing books to persuade you that to deny their thesis is folly. But if their view is correct—if we think what we think and do what we do because of our genes or chemicals in our brain—then there is no point in trying to persuade us of that point of view. If their view is true, what is the point of creating rational arguments to prove it? In fact, if that view is true, those who believe it only believe it because of their genes or chemicals. To put it another way, those who hold this view invariably appeal to our mind, instead of our brain, all the while denying that there is such a thing as a mind.

While there is certainly a connection, there is also a distinction between the mind and the brain. That we often use the terms as synonyms suggests that our minds, or brains, are not operating at their optimum power. This is like confusing our will with our arm. When we will to move something, we use our arm. But they are not at all the same thing. The same is true when we infer that when we think, we use our brain. But our thoughts are not our brains. Rather, our thoughts make up our mind. Of course there is a connection, just as there is between our arm and our will.

My daughter Shannon has a malformed brain. She has a condition known as lissencephaly, which means "smooth brain." She does not have all the ridges that we're used to seeing on normal brains. And Shannon is rather significantly disabled. At three years of age, she cannot speak or feed herself. As she grows older, the distance between what she can do and what others her age can do will only increase. Because she cannot speak, we know very little about the life of her mind. We do not know the depths of her thoughts. It seems likely that they, too, are not on a par with those of her peers. But she does have a mind. She does have thoughts. And that is not the same thing as her brain. She is a joyful child, spending most of her time smiling and giggling. She is happy about something, thinking about something. And she is doing it all with an impaired brain.

The confusion between mind and brain might better be illustrated by the means through which they change. If the brain consists of matter and energy, of chemicals and electrical impulses, and if that is all there is to our thinking, then our thoughts can only be changed by matter or energy. The mind, however, is changed by arguments. When Francis Crick sat down and wrote *Of Molecules and Men*, he did not do so in his laboratory. He did not fiddle with chemical compounds and then spray them on his book to get people to accept his thesis. He did not arrange his words in such a way that the chemicals that make up the ink and paper would persuade us. Instead, he did what I am doing. He used his mind to give instructions to his fingers to write the words that would interact with your mind. In essence, he denied his own thesis in trying to persuade us of it.

But why? Why would those titanic intellects (not big brains) seek to persuade others of a theory that affirms that there is no such thing as rational persuasion? What is to be gained by adopting this theory of knowledge that contradicts itself? Perhaps it is a road to power. Perhaps if we can believe that all we are is chemicals, then we might have hope for making ourselves better. It was the Dow Chemical Company that once advertised itself as bringing "better lives through better chemistry." If depression is only a failure of some gland to produce enough of some substance, then we'll create a substitute in a pill. If our children are bouncing off the walls while we're trying to teach them something, then we'll give them Ritalin and calm them down chemically.

Therein lies the real danger in this system of epistemology. If we are nothing but chemicals and can control our foibles chemically, then who will do the controlling? And who will decide what is a foible and what isn't? The problem with a faulty epistemology is that it destroys all other aspects of a given worldview. We cannot construct, or even discover, moral imperatives if from the outset we affirm that we cannot say, "It is true that such and such is wrong." If our convictions about right and wrong are nothing but chemical reactions, then there is no way for us to test their validity. They are necessarily arbitrary and nonbinding.

Consider the rhetorical and political battles being fought today over the issue of homosexuality. Some argue that if homosexuality is genetically programmed into people, then we may not speak of it as wrong. That is step one in the use of this worldview; it exonerates us of guilt. But if we are nothing but chemicals, even the convictions of those who disapprove of homosexuality are chemically created. If genetic determinism precludes the condemnation of homosexuality, how can we condemn homophobia or any other kind of prejudice? How can we condemn anything, if we are all at the mercy of chemicals?

If we cannot condemn anything, then we also cannot determine what it is we ought to be curing with our use of chemicals or genetic engineering. Do we cure homosexuality or the distaste for homosexuality? Do we cure cancer or do we "cure" the immune system and make it inoperative? If our desire to survive is but a chemical reaction, why follow it? If we decide that curing cancer is a good thing, we do so only because our chemicals or genes told us to. We soon reduce what ought to be merely to what is. And then we have no reason to change anything. Thus, when we begin with a faulty epistemology, or doctrine of knowledge, we move on to a failed ethic, or doctrine of right and wrong, and conclude with a flawed teleology, or doctrine of purpose.

C. S. Lewis, in his trenchant and prophetic little book, *The Abolition of Man*, makes the same argument. When we seek to harness the power of nature in order to control man, we invariably end up with nature once again on top. The more we are convinced that we can control men through chemicals or genetics, the more we have to affirm that there is no person there. If we are only chemicals, we are only chemicals. And chemicals cannot change themselves, and wouldn't know in what way to do so if they could. If we are only brain and not mind, then we cannot think our way out of any problem. We can only wait for the chemicals to change us, and when they do, we still will not know if we have changed for the better. For the concept of "better" has

no place in a chemical universe. We are left with the fact
that whatever is, is.

The better living that we once hoped for through a
better understanding of how our brains work and how our
genes control us, is borrowed. That is, most of us share a
somewhat common idea of what the good is, or what the
good life is. We prefer pleasure to pain, life to death, knowledge to ignorance, and health to sickness. But these preferences are meaningless in a world in which "truth" is affirmed
because of chemical reactions. And without any sort of transcendent source to determine which preferences are better,
what do we do when people disagree? In the former Soviet
Union, religious faith was determined to be a function of a
sick brain. Those who harbored such convictions were sent
to mental hospitals, where they were sometimes given shock
therapy to purge their brains of whatever chemical errors
caused them to embrace those delusions. There the state determined what mental health was, and sought to bring its vision to pass through manipulating the brain.

In Nazi Germany, a flawed theory of genetics determined who was human and who was not. Those who were
deemed genetically inferior had to be put to death, to pu-
rify the gene pool. In America today, genetic screening is
done daily to determine who will live and who will die, not
on the basis of race or religion, but on the basis of genetic
purity, as unborn children who do not measure up are in-
tentionally destroyed. If the naturalists are right, and we are
only physical entities, then such selection cannot be condemned. After all, whether one wishes to kill Jews or unborn babies, that desire is not a sin, because it is rooted in

chemical reactions. However, there is also no reason to do the killing, because there is no hope to improve the world, if our standards of a better world are likewise the result of chemical reactions or genetic control. You cannot speak of genetic inferiority if our standards are genetically determined.

Happily, few people actually push this view to its logical extreme. By the grace of God, there remains a remnant of a biblical worldview at work even in the broader unbelieving culture. That doesn't change the fact, however, that such is the logical end of this view. As with so many of the epistemologies that we will look at, we tend to use those that serve some immediate purpose, and switch to another one when we have a different purpose. Perhaps our most fundamental epistemology is that one need not be consistent and adhere to just one. The purpose most often at hand, as we cast about for a suitable epistemology, is the intense desire to avoid the guilt we feel. When I commit a wrong, it soothes my conscience to think it wasn't really my fault, but rather the fault of my genes or brain chemistry. When I am wronged, however, my desire for justice calls for a different system of thought, one in which men are held accountable for violating transcendent standards of right and wrong. I am to be excused because I am merely physical. But wrongs against me are to be avenged because I bear the image of God. Homosexual acts are the result of genetics, and so are not to be blamed. But calling such acts abominations is a violation of decency, and so must be stopped. Which "crimes" are in which category has become merely a matter of political power.

But we are not merely chemicals. We are not merely the sum total of our genetic makeup. We are beings who are made in the image of God. Part of that image involves spirit, or soul, which includes our thoughts, our desires, and our emotions. When God made man, he formed him out of the dust of the ground. He made our bodies out of chemicals. Understanding the chemical workings of our brain and understanding the operations of genetics are all a part of our calling as God's image-bearing creatures to exercise dominion over the creation. We are called to exercise such dominion, under the authority of the Creator, within the bounds that he has established. But then, God breathed into Adam the very breath of life, something as immaterial as God and as real as God. He made us neither mere bodies, nor even souls in bodies, but bodies and souls together. Our thoughts, desires, and emotions may produce brain waves, chemical secretions, and changes in heart rate, but they are not the same thing. The thoughts themselves, though they are not measurable, are nevertheless real. My sadness over the loss of a loved one may cause some gland to kick into high gear and secrete some sort of chemical. But it is an event outside my brain (the death of a loved one), and my becoming aware of it, that caused the sadness that in turn caused the secretion. Positively, the satisfaction that Crick and Watson must have felt at making their important discovery was as real as the double helix. It was the fruit of an accomplishment, not the fruit of the helix at work. As men they made an important discovery, and as sinful men they went too far and used it to deny the humanity that they know that they have. We are not mice; we are men.

## CHAPTER FOUR

# MISBEHAVING BEHAVIORISTS

Were one to make a list of the things that have shaped the twentieth century, one would surely want to include the transistor, the microprocessor, and perhaps even uranium. Few, I think, would include the slobber of a dog. But perhaps they should. In 1902, a scientist named Pavlov began a series of experiments using dogs, designed to show the relationship between external stimulus and internal response. He would establish a pattern in which he rang a bell and brought some food to the dog (external stimulus). The dog would react, of course, by salivating (internal response). Once the pattern was set, Pavlov discovered that when he rang the bell, but didn't bring any food, the dog would still salivate. This observation served as the launching point for a new understanding of human behavior, called behaviorism.

Behaviorism arrived on the scene at an opportune time. Freud's theory of psychoanalysis had begun to lose its allure among psychologists. Freud seemed almost too abstract, too speculative. What was needed, some argued, was a more scientific way of analyzing human behavior. We needed to start looking not into the murky darkness of the subconscious, but into the light of observable and measurable phenomena. We needed to stop worrying about what happened in early childhood, and see what we could do to correct inappropriate behavior today. Behaviorism fit that bill.

John B. Watson, considered by most to be the father of behaviorism, actually began his own research without any knowledge of Pavlov's experiments. As the results of Pavlov's studies were published around the world, Watson incorporated them into his own thinking. He saw man as essentially a machine, whose behavior could be controlled just as one operated a machine. His dream was that through essentially mechanistic means, man might be made better. If we can only push the right buttons, give the right stimulus, then we will get the response that we are looking for. If we can make a dog salivate by ringing a bell, maybe we can find something to make men do what we want them to do.

Behaviorism had several well-known popularizers, but perhaps none more influential than B. F. Skinner. In 1938 he published *The Behavior of Organisms*, making his case that internal processes, such as a reasoning mind, do not shape our behavior. Rather, he argued, our thoughts, feelings, and actions are the result of external stimuli, of events occurring outside ourselves. Next he made these ideas more accessible to ordinary people in his chillingly titled work, *Beyond Freedom and Dignity*. There he explained his theories without technical jargon. Still more people came in contact with behaviorism by reading Skinner's novel *Walden II*. This work leads the reader on an idyllic journey through a commune that follows Skinner's principles. Skinner reached millions of people. He almost single-handedly put the pop in pop psychology.

Although behaviorism looks more to external causes of our behavior and Freudianism more to internal causes, the two schools do share a common theme—that we are not to be blamed for our actions, for they are ultimately outside our control. The Freudian, to put it somewhat crassly, may say, "I do this because of trauma in my childhood during potty training." The behaviorist says instead, "I do this because my environment has conditioned me to respond this way." Perhaps that helps to explain a part of their appeal. It is better to be a victim than a perpetrator.

While Freudianism gave its practitioners an opportunity to see into the very recesses of the psyche, behaviorism gave its practitioners a promise of power. After all, if our actions are grounded in practices of our parents decades ago, what could we possibly do to change them? But if external stimuli control what we do, then all we need to do to control people is to control the external stimuli. But therein lies the problem. Once again, behaviorism, considered as a system of truth, as a means of determining why we believe things, falls of its own weight. That is, if we believe what we believe because we are conditioned to believe it by our environment, then our belief in behaviorism is only the result of our environmental conditioning. If it is true, we think it is true for no good reason.

Those who believe in behaviorism, however, do not

behave like behaviorists. Pavlov did not ring a series of bells in order to persuade his audience of his views. Watson did not write learned books and articles in scientific journals in the hope that the external stimuli of the feel of the paper and the shape of the letters would cause us to embrace his findings. And B. F. Skinner, whether in his more scholarly work or in his more popular writings, was not constructing a box in which he could control the outside forces and manipulate us into agreeing with him. All three men sought to persuade us of a particular epistemology by using methods that were at odds with it. They appealed to the mind, while denying that it could be the font of our thinking. It would seem that anyone who found Skinner's *Beyond Freedom and Dignity* persuasive would have to reject its tenets because his own environment had not conditioned him to accept it.

The claim that we reach our conclusions on the basis of something other than sound reasoning, on the basis of external reasons, has a long history in our discourse. I have heard this objection to my own views more than most, because quite a few people are familiar with my upbringing. I am committed to the same Reformed faith as my father, who is a well-known proponent of it. So when I am contending for it, someone invariably replies, "You think that way only because that is how you were raised." There may indeed be all sorts of inducements for me to embrace the Reformed faith. If I fail to do so, I will disappoint my father—something I would hate to do. I not only love my father, but also work for him. Were I to embrace Roman Catholicism, my income would take a turn for the worse.

My wife would be upset, as would my friends. My children would think I had gone mad. But when I seek to persuade Roman Catholics to become Protestants, they understand that whatever other inducements there may be to hold one view over the other, the only real issue is what is true. The heart, we are told, has reasons that reason knows not of. But that doesn't mean that we should succumb to those un-reasonable reasons.

The heart that has unreasonable reasons, the Bible tells us, is desperately wicked. We all allow our ideas to be formed by our hearts instead of our minds. We then, be-cause they too are fallen, misuse our minds to defend our wickedness. We have a propensity to believe what we want to believe, sometimes for sinful reasons. In Romans 1, for instance, Paul tells us that through the created order, all men everywhere know that there is a sovereign and tran-scendent God of the universe. Paul also tells us, however, that all men, without the regenerating work of the Holy Spirit, suppress that truth in unrighteousness. We know that God's existence is threatening to us, for he is holy and we are not. To avoid condemnation, we ought to repent, but instead, all too often, we deny the God we know and make our own god. In Paul's language, we worship the crea-ture, rather than the Creator.

On the one hand, this seems to suggest that we don't reach our conclusions in a rational way; instead, the world around us compels us to create false beliefs. On the other hand, it also tells us that we know what we know. All men reason rightly that there is a transcendent God to whom we are accountable, and then we try to pretend that we have

not so reasoned. Our propensity to believe what we want to
believe is real, but not all-powerful. It is an often sinful tendency to be combated, not an inevitability to blithely accept. Because we can combat this tendency, we are judged
by God for failing to believe and act on what we already
know to be true.

The behaviorist epistemology cannot stand. It fails its
own test, for if it is true, we believe it only because of our
environment, and so cannot really know if it is true. It also
fails in many other ways. As a failed epistemology, it must
fail in every other area of inquiry. We cannot construct a
sound ethic from it for two reasons. First, if we believe what
we believe because of our environment, then we believe
what we believe about ethics because of our environment.
So when I assert, "It is wrong to torture animals," I am
merely communicating a message given to me by my environment. I am not communicating anything that is necessarily true. Were I to plunder the home of Dr. Skinner, and
he were to object, all he would be doing is sending the message that his environment taught him to object when he is
being robbed. Worse still, his objections belie the very belief he holds so dear. If he wants to convince me to stop
stealing from him (a wish that is no better and no worse
than the wish that I continue to plunder him), he can only
do so, according to his own system, by changing my environment so that I will no longer want to steal from him.
Worse still, his theories about how to change my environment do not necessarily correspond to reality, for they are
only the responses conditioned by his environment.

The second reason this epistemology fails in the arena

of ethics touches also on teleology, the study of purpose. Remember that one of the compelling features of this system of thought is that it presumably offers far greater power to change our behavior. Many people find this view attractive because it claims to offer the opportunity to stop destructive behavior and encourage productive behavior. But there is the rub. This system cannot offer any way to distinguish between destructive and productive behavior. It cannot determine what kind of environment to build because it cannot determine what kind of men to produce.

Suppose the behavioral psychologists discover that the color blue has a tendency to encourage suicide. Their studies show that all people who commit suicide do so immediately after staring at the color blue. Yellow, they find, gives people a joyful spirit and encourages good will. If such were actual findings, we would naturally want to paint the world yellow and wear tinted glasses, lest the sky and the sea drive us to despair. Such a course of action, however, would make no sense in this system. It only makes sense in a system, such as the Christian worldview, where suicide is determined by a transcendent authority to be wicked and perverse. To the behaviorist, the preference of life to suicide has no objective meaning. It is merely the by-product of our own peculiar environment. The desire for life over death may just be the result of an overexposure to the color purple. The behaviorist's goal is utterly arbitrary. But it gets worse. If our thoughts are merely the conditioned responses that flow from our environmental conditions, we cannot even know that blue makes us sad and yellow makes us happy. Perhaps it was the white in their lab coats that led the behavioral psychologists to conclude that blue makes us sad. Perhaps it is really yellow that makes us sad, and blue that makes us happy, but we reached the wrong conclusion because of our environment.

The system fails because it is an attempt to have the power of the outside while staying on the inside. It claims virtual omnipotence over men by affirming that things outside ourselves cause us to believe what we believe. For that power to be real, however, we cannot step outside of it. If men are controlled by their environment, then the men who seek to control other men by controlling their environment are in turn under the control of their environment. Behaviorists act as though others are under the control of their environment, while they themselves are not.

Behaviorism hits our lives in a host of ways. One of the most glaring inconsistencies is in the arena of television. Every election cycle, a great hue and cry arises over the baleful influence of television, and then music, movies, and video games. From time to time, entertainment executives are called to testify in Washington, to justify the moral sludge they produce. And the dance is always the same. The executives argue that the sludge they produce does not change the behavior of those who swim in it. It's just entertainment, they say. Once they leave Washington, however, the executives sing a rather different song. When dealing with potential advertisers, they argue that a series of well-crafted commercials can change the behavior of millions. An endless stream of sex and violence will have no effect, they argue, but images of an athlete wearing a particular swoosh on his hat will sell millions of pairs of sneakers. They want to have their cake and eat it too.

Sadly, Christians have jumped on one side of this bandwagon, often uncritically. The church has been there, fighting side by side with the cultural conservatives, often arguing like behaviorists. But if we are helpless pawns in the face of degrading entertainment, then how can we hold those in Hollywood accountable for creating it? They also must be helpless in the face of such entertainment, and so cannot be held accountable. It is true that moral sludge is not healthy, that exposing ourselves to temptation, rather than fleeing from it, is utter folly. But it is likewise folly to accept the notion that we are helpless in the face of that temptation. We are too often like Adam, who complained to God, "It was the women you gave to me"—only our fall guy is the television.

Behaviorism also drives our criminal justice system. We no longer place criminals in penal camps. Instead, we place them in rehabilitation centers. That is, our courts no longer administer justice and dole out appropriate punishments for particular crimes. Instead, they seek to heal criminals of their psychological afflictions. We want to create an environment where this healing can take place. On the surface, and according to the rhetoric, such is the modern and compassionate way of dealing with crime. It leaves out any moral condemnation. It is poverty and not sin, we are told, that makes criminals. It is troubled home lives that cause youngsters to become delinquents. There is no shame in crime, for the perpetrator is just another victim.

This kinder, gentler approach to crime, however, is

neither kinder nor gentler. In the first place, it is utterly dehumanizing. It makes automatons of us all, denying that we are responsible moral agents. We are instead mere puppets on strings. Such a view doesn't encourage good behavior. If I am taught that I cannot help what I do, that I am a victim of circumstance, then I will not help what I do, and will continue to do evil. By excusing crime, we are encouraging crime.

There is, however, an even more chilling problem with this approach to dealing with criminals. When a criminal is required to "pay his debt to society," that debt can usually be paid. There is an end in sight to the punishment, at which point justice requires that it stop. An eye for an eye may sound barbaric to us, but it stops the punishment at the eye. If, however, we see crime as a disease, the criminal can be set free only when he is healed. And knowing when someone is healed is less than an exact science. If we guess that he is healed before he is healed, then the poor sick criminal goes and commits more crimes that he is helpless to stop. If we guess that he is healed after he is healed, then he sits in the rehabilitation center long after he should. A man is not treated well when he is treated as a puppet, whether he has committed a crime or not. We must treat criminals as human beings.

Behaviorism has had a profound influence on our culture, beyond the fields of entertainment and justice. We are becoming a nation of victims and whiners. Much of what we call "pop psychology" is built around the premise that we are controlled by our environment. Twelve-step programs of every conceivable kind propagate the disease model of sin. No one, of course, can be blamed for catching a disease. No one can be held accountable when our environment made us do it.

The true appeal of this system is not in its promise of power, but in its promise of a lack of power. It's not that practicing behaviorism will enable us to stop doing wrong, but that believing in it will excuse us for the wrong that we have done. This is the end result of our refusal to affirm what our environment shows us to be so, that there is a holy God that we are failing to obey. We not only fail to worship the Creator, but construct a view of reality in which we cannot be held accountable for our sins. Our knowledge, Scripture tells us, condemns us. And if the only way to get out from under that condemnation is to deny that we have that knowledge, then that is what we will do.

Paul's purpose in telling us in Romans 1 that all men know that there is a God and that they have fallen short of what he requires, is to show us that we are all therefore without excuse. We cannot stand before the judgment seat of God and plead ignorance. We cannot complain that we did not know what he had made abundantly plain. We cannot argue that our environment made us do it, for our environment, the created order of God, told us precisely not to do it.

We are not at the mercy of our environment. We are not mere dogs. We are men and women made in the image of God, who have willfully denied the God who made us. We will not escape his judgment by denying his image in us. Nor will we ever find ourselves "cured" of the disease of sin by being rehabilitated. There is only one way of escape: a repentance that affirms that we are responsible, and a dependence upon the work of Christ.

PART TWO

# THE NEW ICE AGE

## CHAPTER FIVE

# IMPRACTICAL PRAGMATISTS

The term *philosophy*, if we have learned anything thus far, might rightly be accused of being something of a misnomer. Coined by bringing together two Greek words, it literally means "the love of wisdom." What we have seen so far is that far too many philosophers are more lovers of folly than lovers of wisdom. As a field of inquiry, however, philosophy can be broken down into various constituent parts. Our chief concern so far has been with that branch of philosophy known as epistemology, which is the study of knowledge, or how we know things. As we have seen, however, these categories are not completely separate. Epistemology overlaps with ethics, as we saw so clearly with behaviorism. If we believe what we believe because our environment conditions us to believe it, then we cannot rightly say, "It is wrong to commit murder," for our conclusion is dependent upon our environment. We saw also that epistemology affects our teleology, another branch of philosophy, the study of purpose. We cannot know what we are for, or at what we should be aiming, if our conclusions on these matters are merely the product of our environment. One side of the question will always have a profound impact on the other side. So one cannot choose different approaches for different branches of philosophy. I am again loving folly and not wisdom if I assert, "When it comes to epistemology, I am a logical positivist, and when it comes to ethics, I affirm natural law."

Not all philosophy claims to begin with epistemology. In some sense it always must, because epistemology is basic to all our other conclusions. We cannot affirm anything about anything without first understanding how it is that we make affirmations. Nevertheless, when the pre-Socratic philosopher Parmenides set out to explain the nature of reality, his chief concern was metaphysics, not epistemology. His grand assertion, that whatever is, is, has much to say about epistemology, but that was not his goal.

Pragmatism, the focus of our attention in this chapter, likewise did not begin with epistemology. However, it was perhaps the beginning of the slide of modern philosophy into rampant skepticism. If it wasn't the beginning, it was at least a great slip backward into it. Skepticism has roots going back to the days of Socrates. Before his time, the Greek philosophers were engaged in a great struggle between the views of Parmenides and the views of Heraclitus. Parmenides made the history books with that great dictum already quoted, "Whatever is, is." Heraclitus was his nemesis, affirming instead that "Whatever is, is changing." Heraclitus declared that one cannot step into the same river twice, as the river is in a constant state of flux. Such, he argued, was the case with all reality. There is nothing that is not changing, becoming something else. Because both men affirmed part of the truth and missed another part, there would be no peace over the matter.

That failure to reach a consensus gave birth to the first skeptics in the history of philosophy, the Sophists. The Sophists were the first philosophers to self-consciously despise wisdom. They insisted that wisdom cannot be found. Heraclitus had failed, Parmenides had failed, and so had many others before their time. These intellectual giants had sought to probe the nature of the universe and came up empty. Perhaps, the Sophists argued, that was because there was no real wisdom to be found. This school of philosophy, however, did not close up shop and go find something productive to do. Instead, they devoted themselves to the basest forms of rhetoric. If there was no truth to be found and taught, they seemed to reason, then perhaps we should learn how to persuade people through manipulation. Philosophy degenerated into the art of persuasion. Ideas were no longer judged by whether or not they were true, but by the skill with which they were presented. Form not only triumphed over content, but swallowed it up. It was into this situation that Socrates stepped and revived philosophy as the pursuit of wisdom. His pupil, Plato, and Plato's pupil, Aristotle, continued that movement. Each affirmed a metaphysic that could at least in part get past the impasse reached by Parmenides and Heraclitus.

I've taken the time to deal briefly with ancient philosophy to help us better understand the context in which pragmatism became a powerful force in philosophy. Skepticism reared its ugly head several times between the time of Socrates and our own time, each time because of a perceived deadlock in the pursuit of wisdom. When John Locke and René Descartes pushed two opposing epistemologies, and neither side prevailed, David Hume responded with skepticism. But skepticism can have a number of faces. The skepticism of the pragmatists had none of the cynical overtones of the skepticism of the Sophists. On the contrary, it had a decidedly positive and American flavor. Pragmatism has been called the only indigenous American philosophy. Born at the turn of the twentieth century, it was marked by an optimism about mankind's future and our ability to progress. Its earliest and most vocal proponents included Charles Peirce (1839–1914), William James (1842–1910), and John Dewey (1859–1952). Peirce was the founder of this movement, and James and Dewey popularized it and spread its influence into various fields of inquiry. Peirce argued that the best way to judge a given proposition is not to see if it is true, but rather to consider the usefulness of embracing it. If we affirm something, what will the result be?

The history of science illustrates the difference between that which is true and that which is useful. For most of history, it was believed that the earth was the center of the universe. This conviction made it difficult to explain the movement of the stars and planets in the sky. Nevertheless, the ancient astronomer Ptolemy came up with a model that would explain the phenomena. It consisted of a series of spheres within spheres, each carrying various planets or stars. With each sphere postulated to move at a different rate, and each sphere having a different size, Ptolemy mimicked the movements of the heavenly bodies. When Copernicus later argued that the sun is the center of our solar system and that we move around it, rather than it moving around us, the scientific community eventually came to embrace that view. However, because the Copernican model assumed that planetary motion was circular (rather than elliptical), it could not predict the positions of stars and planets in the sky more accurately than the Ptolemaic model. In short, Copernicus's view was "true," but Ptolemy's view "worked." The pragmatist would argue that we should conclude that the universe consists of a series of spheres within spheres, because this model gives us the answers that we need in order to calculate the positions of the stars. But Ptolemy's system is fundamentally false. *True* and *false* are meaningless terms to the pragmatist, however. All that matters is what works and what doesn't work.

This notion appealed to the American mind-set, especially at the turn of the century. We were a practical people, bent on productivity, not idle speculation. We wanted "news we could use." Abstract thinking was pointless nonsense. The pursuit of transcendent truth was a fool's errand. This, then, was more of a nonphilosophy than a philosophy. Perhaps the greatest pragmatic decision of the pragmatists was their decision to spread their wisdom through institutions of higher learning, and later through all educational institutions. The University of Chicago was a pragmatist stronghold in the early days of the movement, but it soon spread. John Dewey moved pragmatism out of the ivory tower and into the playground. He was the most influential thinker in the field of education in his day, and perhaps in all of the twentieth century. He not only taught students this view, but taught students who would one day teach students. His influence spread further as he taught those who would be teaching teachers for generations to come. As pragmatism spread, so did the skepticism that bore it. Dewey affirmed not only that philosophy was devoid of truth, but that there was no truth to be found in any area of inquiry. Education, then, was not the process by which we pass on eternal truths, but rather the process that brings about the results we seek in the rearing of children. The minds of children did not need to be informed, but to be molded and shaped for the greater well-being of the society.

The problem with pragmatism as an epistemology— with deciding that truth should be determined by what works best—is that it just doesn't work. It begins with an impossible teleological hill to climb. It cannot begin to answer the obvious question, "Works for what?" How do we answer this question without already having a true standard of what our goal is?

My son Campbell, who just turned six, recently received a wonderful hand-me-down from his cousin, a sweatshirt bearing the insignia of the Pittsburgh Steelers. My son thinks the Pittsburgh Steelers are the greatest thing since sliced bread, largely because of his epistemology. In short, it is this: "If Daddy believes it, then I believe it." The problem, however, is not his epistemology, but his size. Although he has his father's convictions about the Steelers, he doesn't yet have his father's prodigious belly, and so the sweatshirt is rather large on him, hanging down to his knees. My son also shares with his father a certain sartorial apathy. He's not the kind to check himself in the mirror before he goes out. His mother, my wife, is a little more particular. So when my son waltzes into the room, after he has put on his new sweatshirt, my wife is wont to tell me, "Dear, that shirt is still too big." My response gets at the heart of the pragmatist's problem: "Too big for what?" She then replies, "Too big for Campbell." And I reply, "Too big for Campbell to do what?" She is assuming a common goal, that my son not look silly. But my son and I are more interested in communicating our loyalty to the Steelers than we are in looking normal.

There is no route available to the pragmatist to discover what route we all should be on. In the field of education, if we can all agree that we must base our success or failure on the achievement of certain prescribed outcomes, we are still up in the air in trying to determine what those outcomes should be. When John Dewey first began his assault on the American educational establishment, his goal was rather straightforward. Schools were asked to produce well-ordered young men and women who could contribute to the national economy. We find the same fundamental principle at work in various educational "reforms" being pushed by the educational establishment today. Both outcome-based education and school-to-work systems operate out of the same premise. The same is true for our institutions of higher learning. There was a time once when our colleges and universities existed to create well-rounded, thinking men and women, to equip them with a "liberal" education. By and large, these institutions are now little more than professional training schools.

All that has changed, and that only slightly, is the goals for which we are working. Now the outcomes we seek include not only the capacity to hold down a productive job, but to embrace the worldview of the educational elite. That worldview, however, again cannot be determined to be true through the pragmatic method. If there is no way of determining that life "works" better than death, if there is no transcendent moral standard, then we cannot rightly condemn the rash of school killings that have shocked our nation over the past decade. To assert that it is better that students should not be killed by their peers than that they should be is to borrow a moral standard from a source other than "what works."

Few would make that objection, of course. Most of us do in fact believe that mass killings work worse than no mass killings. But we have no reason to reach that conclusion. The basis for determining what works must always come from an ethical system outside of pragmatism. It can only operate on capital, in this case moral capital, that it borrows from some other source. That source may be the Christian ethic, which affirms that all humans bear the image of God and so must be treated with dignity, and which affirms that life may be taken only in accordance with God's law. Or, that ethic may come from a sinister source. For example, the Nazis called their program of destroying Jews "the final solution." It was in part built on pragmatism, which identified a problem, and then, without regard to morality, posited a solution that would efficiently remove it.

Pragmatism is, in short, amoral. It cannot provide any sort of ethic at all. It has historically tried to adopt the most basic of ethics, survival. Based on an evolutionary model, it suggests that what works is what will best ensure the survival of man as a species. But why? Why is survival better than nonsurvival, on pragmatic grounds? Why does survival work better than extinction? If man is a recent addition to the ecosystem of the earth, as evolutionists suggest, might we not better argue that our extinction works better than our existence? It certainly has a longer track record.

Moving back to pragmatism as an epistemology, we find that it, too, fails its own test. If we should treat only those things that work as true, then we cannot treat pragmatism as true, because it simply does not work.

While pragmatism doesn't work as a coherent system (indeed, there are few professional philosophers today who would try to defend pragmatism as a philosophical system), it does work in the sense that it has proved to be attractive in our age. It has had a profound influence on our culture, and drives not only how we see education, but how we see much of our lives. During the Clinton administration, our nation went through the spectacle of an impeachment. The issue divided the nation, as some hoped to see the President removed from office on the basis of his perjured testimony. For the most part, those defending the President did so, not by denying the accusations of perjury, but by arguing that he should stay in office despite the perjury. At the time, the stock market was rising, unemployment was falling, and budget deficits were disappearing. With the exception of the perjury and the behavior that prompted it, all was well.

Many hoped to see the President weather the storm because things were "working" well. It would, in a pragmatic scheme, be unethical to remove the President from office simply because he did something unethical.

Pragmatism drives one side of another national debate. When President Clinton was first running for president, he announced that it was his intention to make abortion in this country "safe, legal, and rare." Once in office, he jettisoned "rare" as a goal, but even the suggestion that abortion should be rare seems to imply that it is a nasty business. Nobody is proud of abortion or parades it as virtuous. But *Roe v. Wade*, the 1973 Supreme Court decision that made abortion legal throughout the nation, has often been defended by this argument: If abortion is made illegal again, women will be hurt by seeking it out from unscrupulous back-alley abortionists. That follows Peirce's reasoning perfectly well. The question is not whether it is wrong for the state to protect the practice of abortion, but what bad things will happen if we overturn *Roe v. Wade?*

This insidious philosophy, however, influences not only our national debates, but also our personal decision making. In the last chapter, I noted that I believe essentially the same things as my father. My work is done within strong ideological circles. If I were to embrace some other system of doctrine, Christian or otherwise, it would have a profound impact not only on my soul, but on my body. My income would fall through the floor. The very nature of the work that I do would change. But if any of the things I affirm about the Christian faith are not true, then I must abandon them, no matter what the cost. A pragmatic approach would only lead to cynicism and despair. My fear is that all of us make pragmatic decisions about our convictions all the time: If I affirm $x$, I will disappoint my family. If I deny $y$, I will lose prestige in the eyes of my peers. If I believe $z$, then others will be offended, and I will lose my friends.

Pragmatism also fails because it claims an omniscience that it cannot have. Not only can we not determine the good that we should be seeking, but we cannot know the consequences of our ideas. Even if I could know that it is a good thing for the human species to survive, and could reach the conclusion that those things are true which encourage its survival, how can I know what fruit will come forth from what ideas? Consider the case of a Jewish watchmaker who lived nearly two hundred years ago. He and his family prospered, as they served the Jewish community in which they lived and worshiped. Eventually, however, the family decided to move away. They found themselves living not in a Jewish community, but in a Lutheran one. The father no longer had fellow Jews for customers. So he and his family embraced, or at least appeared to embrace, the Lutheran faith. Surely such a decision was a wise one, economically speaking. The family continued to prosper. But the effects of that pragmatic decision were utterly devastating. That family included a son. That son, seeing the sheer hypocrisy of his father's "faith," decided that all religions are false, and that their only function is to manipulate the poor with the promise of future reward. That son, Karl Marx, wrote about those convictions and others when he penned, with Friedrich Engels, *The Communist Manifesto*.

Marx's father did not, and could not, know the future. Had he been able to do so, he would have known that it would have been far more pragmatic on the global scale for him and his family to starve from a lack of business. His crassly commercial decision helped create the bitter worldview of Marxism, which animated the cruelty of Joseph Stalin, the greatest mass murderer in the history of the world.

Even the proclamation of the gospel of Jesus Christ has been turned upside down by pragmatism. We sometimes seek the lost by appealing not to the truth of the faith, but by affirming all the benefits that might come to one who embraces it. "Come to Jesus," the evangelist cries, "and all your troubles will end. You will know nothing but joy and peace." We ask people to believe, not because the message of Christ is true, but because it is good for you. Jesus, on the other hand, took a decidedly different approach. He warned those who were thinking about becoming his disciples to "consider the cost." He reminded them that to be identified with him was to invite scorn and persecution, because servants are not greater than their master.

We are pragmatic about our pragmatism. We don't often affirm it publicly. We only call upon pragmatism when it is pragmatic to do so. When we are confronted with our guilt about this decision or that action, we reason that we did it for the greater good. When we are tempted to compromise our firmest convictions, and we succumb, we soothe our conscience by reasoning that we are only being "practical." But that reasoning overlooks the ultimate consequence of pragmatism, which is far more chilling than the Soviet purges. Pragmatism is impractical because it leads to the consuming wrath of God Almighty. Although God's judgment is yet unseen, it is nevertheless certain. The only safe thing, the only practical thing, is to believe what God says and obey him, no matter what the cost. He will judge the moral cowardice that subjects conviction to the vicissitudes of survival. And he will judge such behavior severely.

## CHAPTER SIX

# SKEPTICAL OF SKEPTICISM

I attended a private high school in Wichita, Kansas. It was a small school, but it had a reputation for solid academics. It had been founded by a friend of my father's. My family did not live in Kansas at the time, but in Pennsylvania. I did reasonably well in my classes, but I was far from a happy camper. I became a walking, hardly ever talking, angry young man. High schools are full of clichés. Rather than become a jock, or a gear-head, or a computer geek, I became the misunderstood, deep-thinking, introspective loner. James Dean was my idol. I dressed in black, wore my hair over my eyes, wrote morbid poetry about walls and masks, and reached the conclusion that only shallow fools could ever be happy. That was my niche, my shtick. I didn't like being away from home, and I decided that the cool thing to do would be to live in despair. I only wish now that I had had the eyes to see then just how comical my earnest rejection of earnestness was.

Soon after I adopted this sophomoric pose, my father

came for a visit. He took me out for dinner. We sat down and he asked me without any preliminaries, "What are you angry about?" He read me loud and clear. I was of course too sullen to give much of an answer. But I clearly remember something he told me during our conversation. "Son," he said, "the fastest and cheapest way to earn a reputation as an intellectual is to adopt the pose of the skeptic." My father is a wise man. He did not scream and shout over my slouching. Neither did he perform like a clown to break through my cheerless façade. Quietly, calmly, he threw down a gauntlet he knew I would have to pick up. He knew I wanted to be thought of as an intellectual. Call me weird, but don't call me shallow. He knew also that I could not stand myself if I knew I had earned the reputation falsely, the easy way. If skepticism was fast and cheap, I wanted no part of it. I cheered up, and found something to be earnest about, something to have convictions about, something to stand for. I became a zealot for the Reformed faith, and haven't looked back.

I recount that rather embarrassing phase of my life to get at one of the things that we find so appealing about skepticism. It is still a rather popular pose, even without the silly haircut. There is, in fact, a kind of mood of skepticism—or worse, cynicism—in our culture. We judge all our experiences with a sort of superior ennui. We expect our politicians to lie to us, and anyone who is shocked receives that most damning of adjectives, naïve. When Bob Dole asked about the indifference to his opponent's history of personal behavior, "Where is the outrage?" he showed himself to be hopelessly out of touch. Outrage requires conviction, and conviction is in short supply in our day. Our mood is well summarized by the quip, "Been there, done that, got the T-shirt." We are not outraged by our lack of outrage. We are too full of ennui to be concerned about our ennui. We yawn our way through life, lest we be accused of being earnest. Our zeitgeist is spiritless.

Skepticism, however, is more than a mood or an attitude. It is more than a temporary phase of jaded youth. At its root, skepticism is an epistemology, or rather the beginning of the denial of epistemology. Skepticism grows, as we saw in the last chapter, out of a crisis of belief. When our fundamental presuppositions are challenged, our tendency is to recoil from committing to any conclusions. Modern skepticism grew not only out of a deadly philosophical impasse, but also out of sweeping challenges to long-held beliefs about our world. When Columbus discovered the New World, he also challenged the assumptions of the Old World. And as soon as we absorbed the idea that the earth was round, Copernicus showed that our planet was not the center of the universe. Our cosmology had to change. Our understanding of man had to change.

In the meantime, the Renaissance, particularly in southern Europe, began to challenge the accepted wisdom of the Middle Ages. No longer would men be dependent upon revelation and church dogma for their conclusions. Skeptics were skeptical first about God's revelation to man. Locke and Descartes, as we mentioned in the last chapter, posited new ways of knowing, but their views were never reconciled. Scottish philosopher David Hume pronounced "a pox on both their houses," and became the preeminent skeptic of his day. His skepticism went well beyond that of his predecessors, who wanted human reason to lead the way. He affirmed that reason was a dead end. His skepticism cut to the root of our knowledge. He even attacked the idea of causality.

Hume believed that almost all of our ideas about the world around us come out of our understanding of causality. Yet he denied that we could truly know that one cause brought to pass a particular effect. In logic, we are wary of falling into the informal fallacy of *post hoc ergo propter hoc* ("after this, therefore because of this"). We commit this fallacy when we reason this way: "This morning I put on a blue shirt. I had a very productive day today. Therefore, blue shirts increase productivity." This is an obviously fallacious argument, for there is no discernible connection between the color of my shirt and my productivity. The two facts are merely coincidental, without a causal relationship. Hume asserted that, as far as we could know, all of our conclusions about causality are similarly fallacious, that whenever we say that A caused B, we are jumping to conclusions. When the cue ball hits the eight ball, and the eight ball moves across the pool table, we don't really see exactly how the motion of one causes the motion of the other. There is no discreet moment or event when the actual cause takes place.

This view goes against our common sense. We know from observation that eight balls do not move by themselves. We know all about inertia—that bodies at rest tend to remain at rest, and bodies in motion tend to remain in motion, unless acted upon by an outside force.

Hume, however, never denied that some things cause other things. The issue ultimately was not about causality, but about epistemology. Hume argued that we cannot know for certain what causes what. There was, in his mind, a disjunction between the outside world and the world of our minds. How can we know that what we observe is in fact real? Isn't it possible that at the precise moment when the cue ball stops and the eight ball begins its journey, God places his hand upon the one and pushes the other? We cannot step outside ourselves into the outside world, and still know something inside ourselves. As the result of this reasoning, Hume wrote in the conclusion to Book I ("Of the Understanding") of A *Treatise of Human Nature*: "I am ready to reject all belief and reasoning, and can look upon no opinion even as more probable or likely than another."

Hume's radical skepticism had a profound impact upon all of Europe. The breezy acceptance of empiricism that drove so much of scientific inquiry was shattered. Thomas Reid, leader of the Scottish common-sense realists, replied to Hume that anytime philosophy leads us away from common sense, we know that something is wrong with our philosophy and not with our common sense. We know the cue ball makes the eight ball move, and so we must reject any epistemology that questions it. Immanuel Kant responded differently. He spoke of Hume as the one who awakened him from his dogmatic slumbers. Kant wanted to honor the insight of Hume, but allow for the possibility of knowledge. Kant sought at least to alleviate the problem of skepticism by positing a different kind of cos-

mology. He argued that the world was divided into two
parts, which he called the phenomenal realm and the
noumenal realm. The phenomenal realm contains all those
things that we perceive with our senses, the phenomena.
They consist of the impressions placed on us by the outside
world. These things are in fact knowable, according to
Kant, and so we can thank him for not being a total skeptic. What we know, however, is limited. For what is not in
the phenomenal realm, but in the noumenal realm, is "the
thing in itself," the real essence of what it is we think we
are experiencing in the phenomenal realm. What we experience is real, but it is not the real thing, so to speak. Perhaps most importantly, God was relegated to the noumenal
realm by Kant. He did not deny God's existence, but only
that God was knowable.

The chasm separating these two realms, according to
Kant, is uncrossable. While there are things in the noumenal realm, we who reside in the phenomenal realm do
not have access to them. In a sense, Kant echoes the in-
spired wisdom of the apostle Paul, who wrote,

> For the wrath of God is revealed from heaven
> against all ungodliness and unrighteousness of men,
> who suppress the truth in unrighteousness, because
> what may be known of God is manifest in them, for
> God has shown it to them. For since the creation of
> the world His invisible attributes are clearly seen,
> being understood by the things that are made, even
> His eternal power and Godhead, so that they are
> without excuse. (Rom. 1:18–20)

Paul too seems to suggest that there is a seen world and an unseen world, the unseen being transcendent over the seen. But the disagreement is critical. Kant says we can learn nothing about the unseen world from the seen, while Paul, under the inspiration of the Holy Spirit, says not only that we can learn such things, but that we do, every one of us. Such knowledge of the transcendent realm is inescapable, Paul says, so that all men are without excuse.

Kant's legacy is seen not only in rank skepticism, but in such later schools of thought as logical positivism. We have already dealt with their empirically unverifiable conviction that only those propositions which can be empirically verified have any meaning. This is akin to saying that we can know things about the observable world, but any claim about anything beyond this world is necessarily nonsense.

Kant, like all skeptics, contradicts himself. Even to begin to speak of the unknowable realm is to speak with a forked tongue. Epistemology itself is not something that we experience with our senses. Kant's whole exposition of his view contradicts that view. He is speaking of knowledge as a thing in itself when he says that it is not knowable. In addition, we most certainly know things about God, even in Kant's own scheme. We know where God lives, his address. If we know that he inhabits the noumenal world, we know that he is transcendent and that he is not given to phenomenal displays. If we know we cannot perceive him empirically, are we not saying that he is invisible, as well as inaudible and untouchable? Indeed, we not only know something about the God who inhabits this unknowable realm, but also something about this unknowable realm it-self—namely, what is there and what is not there.

Hume committed essentially the same fallacy. His skepticism was broader than Kant's, but no more sensible. In order to claim that one cannot know anything, one must claim to know something, namely, that one can know nothing. In fact, in order to claim that one cannot know anything, one would have to know everything. "No truth is knowable" is what in logic is called a universal negative statement. Particular negatives are not so difficult to assess. If I say, "This page is not green," all I need to do to determine the truth or falsity of the statement is to examine this very page. Unless the printer made a bizarre mistake, this page is not in fact green. To demonstrate that "No green pages exist" is false would require only one green page. To demonstrate that it is true, however, would require exhaustive knowledge of every page of paper in the entire universe. In short, I would need universal knowledge. It makes little difference whether we are talking about green pages or something as abstract as truth. To deny that such a thing could exist is to claim to know all that there is about existence.

Skepticism cannot stand up to its own standard. It is a claim to know some truth to say that we cannot know any truth. But there is a great deal of practical hypocrisy as well. Like our other philosophers, skeptics publish books on their skepticism. They not only affirm that truth is unknowable, but they seek to persuade us of their view. They write learned treatises denying that there can be learning. They despair of knowledge and seek to persuade us to share that despair. That is, they not only affirm that no affirmation can be shown to be true, but they try to show us that it is true that no affirmation can be shown to be true. Hume's honest and poignant statement quoted above from *A Treatise of Human Nature* is utterly superfluous. Does he actually want us to believe that he looks at every view as no more probable than any other? If he does, why should we not just as well believe that he believes that some views are more probable than others? Is it not equally probable (indeed, it might very well be true) that in writing the book, Hume might persuade people that he is full of poppycock? If Hume has wisdom, then is it not equally probable to say that he is a fool? If there is a consistent skeptic in this world, and I would be loathe to deny that, for that would be a universal negative, we will not be hearing from him. He would not be making the case for not making cases.

In making the case for skepticism, skeptics not only deny their own epistemology, but also deny their morality and teleology. The fact that they write these skeptical tomes suggests they think it is a bad thing to believe that truth is knowable and a good thing to believe that truth is unknowable. But if it is no better to believe that which is true than that which is false, then why try to change anyone's mind? Indeed, why do anything? Teleology is destroyed by skepticism, for if we cannot know what is true, then we cannot know the true end for which we ought to be striving. Even when the skepticism is limited, even if the skeptic is only skeptical about abstract matters and spiritual issues, then we are still in the same wandering boat. Teleology is not something we learn about empirically. There are no "shoulds" or "oughts" that we see with our eyes. Kant can't find which way to turn without first making a trip to the noumenal realm, and, according to his own thinking, you can't get there from here. Skepticism cannot stand for the very reason that it tries to stand. It affirms the truth that we cannot be certain of any truths. It affirms a morality that says it is wrong to affirm. And it seeks an end that it denies can be knowable.

Skepticism as a philosophy sits aloof from our everyday lives. One won't find too many people riding the bus reading Hume's *A Treatise of Human Nature*. But it is not merely a mood, an intellectual posture designed to feign sophistication. It also lives in that middle ground where people actually make decisions about things. It stops the process by which we seek to be deliberate about all that we do. Why stop and figure out if we should do something, if we know from the start that we can never really figure it out? Why bother to examine a certain truth claim, if we know that no truth claim can be demonstrated? The existential difficulty is that skepticism is existentially difficult. It is a real-life hardship not to be able to reach any definitive conclusions about anything. We find ourselves in despair because—as creatures made in the image of God, designed to actually know things and to think God's thoughts after him—we long not only to find answers to our heartfelt questions, but also to believe that such answers are knowable. How can we trust our spouse, if we cannot really know if our spouse is trustworthy? That's not a philosophical question, but a human one. How can we know that the work we do has real and last-

ing meaning when we know that we cannot know anything for certain?

Here is where an epistemology built on the revelation
of God can not only silence the philosophers, but also provide comfort. Our worldview not only has philosophical
answers, but also has answers for all those seemingly unan-
swerable questions that grow out of our own skewed thinking. We, all of us, the lost and the found, were made in
God's image. As such, we hunger for the same things. But
if we have been remade in the image of the Son, we know
where to find the food that is food indeed.

Our job is to answer the skeptic at all three levels. To
the philosopher, we demonstrate that if he is to believe in
his skepticism, he must first deny his skepticism. We answer
the skeptic with the skeptic, and show him to be a fool. For
the jaded, we gladly live our lives in earnest, being willing
to be thought of as fools for the sake of Christ. We are not
ashamed of the gospel, for to believe it is life, abundant life.
And to the despairing, we offer the truth: that we can and
do know things, that God in his grace has revealed things,
and that God has revealed the grace of Christ. He has given
us truth in his Son. He has given us the good in his Son.
And he has given us an end, a direction and a purpose, in
his Son.

Tragically, the spirit of skepticism has found its way
into the church. We don't deny that we can know anything, but too often we treat the Scriptures as Hume treated
the whole world. It is too complex, too abstruse, we seem to
reason, to reach any real conclusions. That argument actually preceded Hume. It was the Roman Catholic humanist

Erasmus who argued that Scripture is too lofty to be understood. His polemical opponent was the hero of the Reformation, Martin Luther. Luther's response to Erasmus was as simple as it was profound: "Spiritus Sanctus non est skepticus" ("The Holy Spirit is not a skeptic"). If the Spirit has given us life, then we should not be skeptics, either.

## CHAPTER SEVEN

# RELATIVELY RELATIVIST

T he serpent, we are told, was more crafty than any other beast. His pitch began with subtlety. He knew better than to start with a full frontal assault. Eve, after all, though she may have been born yesterday, was no fool. Her mind was not burdened with the foolishness that she would bequeath to her children and her children's children. The serpent had to be careful, and so he was. He began with a simple question: "Has God said . . . ?" He did not begin by denying what God had said. Rather, he began by planting a seed of doubt. The doubt was fed by what followed: "You may not eat of any of the trees of the garden?" No, God had not said that. Perhaps the serpent was trying to get Eve to believe that somehow God had been less than generous, or less than fair. If, after all, one cannot eat of the best tree, what good is it to be able to eat from the other trees? Eve's faith seemed to stand firm, but it did not. She corrected the devil's misunderstanding of the law of God. "No," she said, "we may eat of any of the trees of the garden, save one." But then she slipped, and added to God's law. "But of the tree of the knowledge of good and evil, we may not eat, nor may we touch it." Did God say not to touch it? He said no such thing. Already Eve had joined the serpent on the sandy ground of affirming that God had said what he had not said. "If we eat of that tree," she continued, "we shall die." Eve correctly remembered the sanction that God had placed on his covenant with man. Then the devil said those words that should have ended his plans, "You shall not surely die." There was a flat contradiction to the plain word of God. God said A, and the devil said *non-A*.

The devil took that chance of being direct with Eve because of what he had next for her: "For God knows that in the day you eat of it your eyes will be opened, and you will be like God, knowing good and evil" (Gen. 3:5). Motive is important. Perhaps you've been in a conversation in which a person you respect has been accused of doing something wrong. You probably had a hard time taking the charge seriously, both because of your knowledge of that person and because you didn't see what he could have gained by doing it. There has to be a motive, or we won't believe it. Here, Satan provided a motive. He told Eve that God had said what he said out of jealousy, not wanting to share his glory with another. Satan not only ascribed a motive to the Almighty, but also provided a powerful incentive to Eve. Of course she would want to be more like the God she loved. The true craftiness, however, was in providing an incentive that was not too grandiose. Eve, still unencumbered by the effects of the Fall on the mind, would probably have laughed in the devil's face, were it not for an important qualifier in his promise. He told her that if she ate of the forbidden tree, she would be *like* God. He couldn't promise her that she would be God. Eve, as an unfallen creature, no doubt knew that not even God himself could make her God. Neither a piece of fruit nor God himself can create an uncreated being. And so the devil promised something less, that she would be like God.

Today, however, the devil is no longer dealing with unfallen creatures. In fact, the second time he tried to tempt an unfallen person, this time in a barren wilderness, he failed miserably. We, however, no longer have the intellectual acumen we once had. The devil no longer needs to be quite so crafty, for we are now dupes. The temptation of relativism is as foolish as it would have been to promise Eve that she would be God. The difference is that we have, as a culture, fallen for it—hook, line, and sinker. The promise of relativism is not the promise to know good and evil, but to create it. It is not the promise to make us wise, but to give us the power to make wisdom.

Allan Bloom wrote a powerful exposé of the American university system that became a surprise bestseller in 1987. In *The Closing of the American Mind*, the esteemed professor at the University of Chicago let out the dirty little secret of higher learning, that in the hallowed halls of learning, students were being taught that there is no such thing as objective truth. Institutions ostensibly committed to passing on abiding truth to the next generation instead focused their efforts on confirming what the students believed when they entered college. Bloom claimed that on any given college campus, 98 percent of entering freshman doubt that there is any such thing as objective truth. They enter as relativists and have that relativism confirmed over the space of four years. Apparently it takes an educated person to reach the conclusion that there is no such thing as education. Although Bloom's book sold amazingly well, his concerns have been essentially ignored. Relativism is still dominant on college campuses across the nation and across the whole Western world.

Relativism is much like skepticism, but with two important and closely related distinctions. Skeptics do not deny that there is truth as such—objective truth that is true whether we believe it or not. They merely assert that we can never really know whether what we believe corresponds to reality or not. One might say that metaphysically or ontologically they believe that there is such a thing as the real, but, as with Kant, we can't get there from here. There is no bridge from the world outside us into our minds. Relativists share with skeptics a skepticism about knowing objective truth, but for an altogether different reason. They argue that we cannot know objective truth because it does not exist. It is not unlike the distinction between an agnostic, who says we cannot know if God exists, and an atheist, who says that we can know that God does not exist. In one sense, relativists are more dogmatic than skeptics, because they believe it is certain that there is no certainty. In another sense, they are less dogmatic, because they deny that there is any dogma that has real truth.

The second distinction, however, is a little more confusing, and it brings us back to the devil in the garden. The relativist does affirm that there is truth, but it is only relative truth. It is not what Francis Schaeffer used to call "true truth." The connection back to the devil is this: Because truth is relative to each person, according to the relativist, we do become like God. That is, while we do not and cannot create an objective universe in which others must live, we can, and ultimately must, create our own world. We cannot say, "The moon is made of green cheese," in the sense that you have a duty to believe that it is made of green cheese. But we can say, "The moon is made of green cheese to me," and because all of "reality" is my own construction, there is nothing that anyone can do to undo that conviction. It is true for me. We become as God, creating our own little universe.

The devil has attacked God's truth throughout history. The father of lies doesn't change his stripes. As we have looked at various attempts to construct epistemologies that deny God his rightful place, we have seen the devil continue to ask, "Has God said . . . ?" The difficulty, as we have seen, is that the devil's alternatives just do not work. God says that he made man from the dust of the earth. The devil says that we have descended from single-celled organisms that just happened to form one day in the primordial soup. The more we look at the devil's claims, the more we see that they do not hold water. And so his tack now is relativism. If his truth can't beat God's truth, at least he can deny the possibility of truth. Instead of holding up the counterfeit and trying to pass it off as the real thing, he argues that there is nothing real. Instead of attacking God's truths, he just attacks the idea of truth. Instead of propounding an alternative vision of reality as truth, he argues that no vision of reality is objectively true—not his or anyone else's (including God's).

That is how our culture has moved from modernism, with its various scientific models for discovering truth, to postmodernism, with its often gleeful denial of any truth at all, save the relative truth that inhabits our minds. On the surface, it seems like a bad deal, a step backward for Western culture. What could a culture gain by giving up truth? It gains a façade of peace and, with it, a façade of humility. In the battle between God's view of the world and the devil's, at least it works out to a tie.

Wars, both literal and figurative, are fought over competing truth claims. Whether it is two children fussing back and forth—"Did not!" "Did too!"—or two nations bombing each other over a territorial dispute, we find ourselves disagreeing. With only ourselves to serve as the final arbiters, with no source of infallible truth, we settle our arguments through battle. Wouldn't it be better if my daughter Darby said to my son Campbell, "To me, you shoved me," and he replied, "To me, I did not shove you," and they agreed to disagree? Wouldn't it be better if the Germans said to the Poles, "To us, that region belongs to us," and the Poles replied, "To us, it belongs to us"? That approach will not settle disputes, but it's the modern way to be sure that they don't get out of hand. Children and nations alike can pat themselves on their collective backs for their laudable humility. Neither is making an exclusive claim of truth. Neither is suggesting that the other's view is wrong, only that it isn't true for them. No one arrogantly suggests that he has cornered the market on truth. And, as both sides agree to disagree, swords are beaten into plowshares.

Such is the devil's bargain, and, as with all his bargains, we always lose what we offer in the trade, and never get what he has promised us. He claims that we will be cultivating the virtue of humility and enjoying the blessings of peace, but are we? Suppose Campbell has shoved Darby. And suppose that I explain to Darby that while it seems to her that he did, it seems to him that he didn't. What is to stop my son from shoving my daughter again? What is to stop my daughter from returning the favor, and explaining to me that while to Campbell she broke a vase over his head, to her she didn't? The humility that we thought we gained also removed objective guilt from the equation (which, by the way, is the real reason why relativism is so popular in our day). We thought we had peace, with each child living in his or her own private world. The problem is that in the real world, private worlds intersect. My daughter and my son can't both have what they want. Similarly, while Germany and Poland may agree to disagree whether a particular region belongs to one country or the other, that agreement will break down when both countries try to enforce their laws and collect their taxes there. Our little worlds are not so little that they don't meet up with other little worlds. We can't agree to disagree when we finally have to act. If the right way to go is south to you and north to me, an agreement to disagree will not make the car move. The promised peace slips away.

Relativism not only fails to make peace, but also, like all the other epistemologies we have looked at, fails its own test. When we apply its most fundamental premise to the most fundamental premise, we find that it contradicts itself. Although it is by far the most dominant epistemology of our time, it is clearly and immediately self-contradictory. When I speak on the subject to college students, I give them a three-word refutation of this view. "If one of your professors, or even one of your friends, ever makes the claim that there is no such thing as objective truth," I tell them, "ask them this question: 'Are you sure?' "

Now the relativist is caught on the horns of a dilemma. If he affirms that he is sure, he is affirming an objective truth, namely, that there is no such thing as objective truth—which denies his claim that there is no such thing. But if he denies that he is sure, then he must give up his claim. It is that simple. Relativists can obfuscate all they want, switch the words around, or find a more sophisticated way to make the same point, but the same rejoinder will reduce the premise to rubble. The harder they argue for the truth of their view, the more they prove that there is indeed an objective truth. They want to have their cake and eat it too—or rather, to have their truth and deny it too.

If this view is as foolish as I say it is, why would anyone want to affirm it? What could possibly be the motive? Often there are two motives, the stated motive and the real one. I'm sure there are those who embrace this folly out of that desire we talked about earlier, a sincere desire for peace. Most, however, affirm epistemological relativism because of its connection to moral or ethical relativism. You can understand the two separately, though if you have the former, you will always have the latter. A logical positivist, for instance, could affirm that we can know those truths that are empirically verifiable, and so not be an epistemological relativist. But because issues of ethics cannot be determined through the use of our senses, the positivist might embrace ethical relativism. The person who begins with epistemological relativism, however, must end with ethical relativism. One cannot say at the same time that there is no objective truth and that it is objectively true that certain actions are ethical or unethical.

I made this point clear one morning while teaching a class at the University of Mississippi. I had a student who blurted out from the back of the classroom, "There is no objective truth." I replied, "You get an F in this class for the semester," and went on about the business of the class. All the students were horrified, and the bold relativist soon piped up, "That's not fair!" I explained to him that I wasn't giving him the F because he deserved it for saying something so foolish. Rather, I said, I was giving him the F just because I wanted to—and then I turned my attention back to the rest of the class. By now, though, the rest of the class wasn't much interested in the essay we were considering. They wanted to hear the conversation between me and the now red-in-the-face relativist. "You can't do that!" he finally blurted out. "I'll complain to the administration." I smiled at the freshman, and asked him on what basis he would make his complaint. Hadn't he just denied that there was an objective standard of justice? How could he complain if there was no such standard? If I decided to hand out grades on the basis of the amount of cash given to me by my students, there could be no foundation for a complaint if there were no foundation for anything. Thankfully, he abandoned his view and passed the course.

It is not only students, however, who make such foolish mistakes. I was teaching the class while trying to earn a graduate degree in English. So when I wasn't a teacher, I was a student. My zeal for exposing the folly of relativism wasn't limited to my classroom, and I often made the same kinds of arguments in the classes I was taking. The higher-ups began to take notice, and tried to reason with me. I was called into the office to visit with the grand old man of the English department. It was not a meeting I was looking forward to. I was all of 22, a lowly graduate student stepping into the inner sanctum of the august scholar. He invited me to sit down and began to inquire as to my plans. "Is it your hope, young man," he asked me, "to eventually earn a Ph.D. here and then to move on to a teaching career in the university?" I explained that those were indeed my plans. He conceded that I had so far done good work in my studies, but expressed his concern over my habit of speaking of things in "black and white" terms. He graciously warned me that this insistence on looking at things in terms of good and bad, right and wrong, might damage my career prospects. It wasn't a threat, but a kind warning that my views were out of accord with the profession as a whole. As much as I appreciated the warning, I couldn't resist taking the opportunity to expose the folly. "I see, Professor. You're saying that it's not good for me to keep insisting on seeing things in terms of right and wrong?" "Yes," he replied, apparently gratified that I was finally beginning to understand. "I shouldn't keep talking about this kind of thing in class?" "Yes," he replied again, still missing the challenge. Finally I decided to make it easier for him: "So you are saying it is wrong for me to keep talking about right and wrong?" The professor leaned back in his chair, and muttered, "Yes, yes, relativism is a problem. You are excused."

With a foundation of epistemological relativism, no teleology can stand either, and again for the same reasons. If we cannot say that anything is objectively true, we cannot say that it is objectively true that we should be seeking any particular goal. We cannot come up with an overarching goal for mankind or for ourselves. We cannot even come up with small, immediate goals. If we cannot answer moral questions on which people disagree, because truth is relative, how can we decide that it is better for mankind to survive than not to survive? How can we decide whether we should eat a dozen doughnuts for lunch, or cottage cheese and a banana, when we cannot say that it is better to live than to die, or that it is better to be healthy than sick? How can we even define health or sickness? If we cannot know, then we cannot know what to do, or why to do it. Knowledge is necessary for such issues, yet it is impossible in the relativist system.

The relativist is ultimately a solipsist, though an inconsistent one. Solipsism is the idea that only the self exists. Nothing in the world has any objective reality, on this view, but is merely a product of one's own mind. When I turn my eyes down to the computer screen, and stop looking out the window, the entire universe disappears, only to reappear when I raise my head again. Understand that this is not mere skepticism. It's not that I cannot know that the world outside my window exists, but that it ceases to exist when I cease to think it exists. However, our worlds still collide. Sometimes I challenge relativists this way: "To me, you are no longer a relativist. You may no longer deny the truth of objective truth. If I create my reality, I will create one in which I do not create my own reality, and one in which reality is not only outside me, but knowable." My solipsism thus swallows the other guy's solipsism.

Relativism is never more popular than when it touches on that most sensitive of subjects, religion. Our most passionate, and often most deadly, battles flow out of disagreements about who God is. Relativists, however, do not believe in God. They believe in a rather pathetic substitute known as "God-to-me." You will hear them saying things like, "God-to-me is full of love and compassion, and only wants what's best for us all the time." "God-to-me is like an ocean full of love and life, holding me, but never directing me in the way I should go." There are all sorts of things we could talk about in God-to-me theology—how God-to-me almost always looks an awful lot like me, or how God-to-me is almost never an avenging or jealous god. But the strangest thing about God-to-me is his or her origin.

When we read about ancient cultures, we often find ourselves having to labor in order not to laugh. What kind of superstitious rube would take a piece of wood, or gold and silver, shape it with his own hands, and then bow down and worship it? We're far more sophisticated in our age. We do not bow down to things we make with our hands. No, we bow down to things we make with our minds. The ancient idolaters understood that the god they worshiped wasn't inside the statues they made. The statues merely served as tools for worship. We, on the other hand, concede that we have created our ostensive creator with the very name that we bestow on him. Our god's name is a contradiction in terms. Whatever God is, he certainly isn't "God-to-me." Whatever God is, he surely preceded me, and didn't proceed from me. We admit we made the whole thing up, and then base our lives on what we have made up. We are indeed a sad people.

Thankfully, such could never happen in the evangelical church—or could it? An evangelical, historically understood, is someone who affirms that one must believe the evangel, the gospel of justification by faith alone, in order to have peace with God. Now, however, polls show that over half of those who call themselves evangelicals also believe that there is no such thing as objective truth. There is a contradiction. What possible appeal could such a noxious doctrine have to those inside the church? That brings us back to the devil's pitch for this foolishness. It looks humble to concede that what you affirm is not necessarily true for everyone else. And Jesus wants us to be humble. Humility is one of the great virtues. Micah the prophet says that we are to walk humbly with our God (Mic. 6:8). We want to be meek like Jesus.

However, biblical humility doesn't mean saying, "To me Jesus is the Son of God and the Savior of sinners." Biblical humility means bowing before the truth of God, and negotiating it with no one, for no reason. It is pride which, fearful that others might think us narrow-minded, offers up the gospel as one alternative among many. It is humble to say with our Lord, "Repent or perish," and prideful to turn him who is the Truth into merely "Truth-for-me."

The world says that we who affirm that Jesus Christ is the only way, the only truth, and the only life, are arrogant, loveless, and judgmental. Those accusations sting, in part, because we are arrogant, loveless, and judgmental. But it is pride that causes us to avoid those accusations by distancing ourselves from the truth. Humility means being willing, like Jesus, to be persecuted for the sake of righteousness, being willing to be thought proud because we feed upon the truth and will not eat the devil's mock humble pie. We are sinners, and so we should be humble about ourselves. We err in our thinking and in our doing. We are a jumble of sins and lies. But we are called to boast in Christ. If, because we have drunk of the wine of folly that is relativism, we will not confess Christ before men as the only way of salvation, then he will not confess us before the Father.

## CHAPTER EIGHT

# NOTHING BUT NOTHING

I f all that we have considered so far is true, it would seem that those who seek to build a cogent and coherent epistemology are now left with nothing. And some have come to embrace the nothing. Some have realized that something which is merely true for me, but not universally true, is in fact devoid of any truth, and thus ultimately worthless.

Relativism's most sophisticated adherents have thus come perilously close to nihilism. Nietzsche, Sartre, and Camus all held to a view known as existentialism. Existentialism gets its name from its most fundamental assertion, that existence precedes essence. That is, *that* we are is the first truth, and *what* we are is entirely up to us. Happily, there is nothing to constrain us, but, sadly, there is nothing to direct us as to what we should become. Sartre and Camus responded to the emptiness and meaninglessness of human existence with despair. These men mourned the loss of meaning that their own philosophy had created. They suffered from deep angst over their necessary loneliness. They conceived of a universe that was hostile in its indifference. And they spread the word of their despair through literature, each of them writing not only technical philosophical volumes, but also fiction designed to convey their wisdom. These men argued that the only way to be "authentic" is to recognize one's pitiful condition and then determine one's essence, deciding what one will become and what one's purpose will be. That choice, of necessity, has to be random. There are no transcendent standards by which to judge one's choices. The only thing that matters is that you make the choice and know that you make the choice.

Nietzsche, who preceded the others, came up with his own bit of wisdom as to how we should make those choices. He readily conceded that because there was no transcendent truth, there was of necessity no transcendent morality. What we needed, in his view, was a superman, what he called in German the *Übermensch*. This was a man who would rise above the herd and become a master over all things—indeed, a master over other men. Nietzsche condemned Christianity and its ethic as weak and foolish. Some have suggested that it was Nietzsche who laid the groundwork for the rise of Hitler. He derided the Christian ethic as dehumanizing, with its emphasis on mercy and loving one's enemies. He offered in its place the master morality, characterized by what he called the "will to power." Man's purpose is not the survival of the species, not progress as a whole, but for some men to rise above the rest. Nietzsche saw men like Alexander the Great, Julius Caesar, and Napoleon as models of this will to power, and the barbarians who pillaged the Roman Empire as the height of human achievement.

He championed what he called "dialectical courage." This was courage exhibited even with the knowledge that there was no reason to value courage over cowardice. Nietzsche's life, however, did not end with a great show of courage. He spent the last ten of his fifty-six years in an insane asylum, much of it persuaded that he was Jesus Christ. It is said that his sister sold tickets to show people the great mind of Europe at its pathetic end.

Nihilism is the end of the road, because it is the literal antithesis of truth. It is the denial of all virtues, a denial that must inevitably come when the font of those virtues is denied. Our critiques of the various pretenders to the throne of Christ have demonstrated the internal inconsistencies of each of these systems. We will soon look at the inconsistencies inherent in this system. But before we bury Nietzsche, we should praise him. Nihilism, alone among all the systems that we have looked at, recognizes the folly of trying to construct a system of knowledge outside the all-knowing God. It alone has recognized the futility of trying to discover moral law, while denying the existence of the lawgiver. It alone looks at the ugliness of meaninglessness and says that it is ugly. It does not succumb to the almost comical naïveté of the humanist. The humanist affirms, with the nihilist, that we are merely a cosmic accident, the product of purposeless evolution. The humanist affirms, with the nihilist, that of dust we are made, and to dust we shall return, forever. The difference is that the humanist has the audacity to describe man as the highest good. We begin as nothing. We end as nothing. But in between, while we draw breath, we are something special.

Nihilists will have nothing to do with such nonsense. They see the contradiction inherent in that view and reject it out of hand. They simply trudge on, grimly facing grim reality. It is, however, the very grimness of their faces that demonstrates the contradiction in this view. Their sadness over the loss of meaning is a sure sign that they don't really believe there is no meaning. If, for instance, I were to check in my pocket and discover that a penny is missing, I would not grieve over the loss. A penny is virtually worthless. If, however, I could not locate a cashier's check for $1,000,000, I would surely mourn its loss. Similarly, to mourn the loss of meaning is to ascribe great value to meaning. One would not be sad over losing something that one never had. One would not, in fact, have any emotional response. A true nihilist cannot love anything, for to do so would be to value it. He cannot hate anything, either, for to do so would be to value something else. He cannot prefer one thing over another, for that would affirm that one thing is more valuable than another.

Nietzsche preferred courage over cowardice, the master morality over the slave morality. He denied that there could be a transcendent morality, yet the next minute he was vilifying one morality and praising another. He judged Christian morality as dehumanizing, but that placed a value on that which is human. He was in fact affirming the Christian view that human beings are endued by their Creator with dignity. Nihilists affirm that there is no objective standard of right and wrong, but because such a view is utter nonsense, they cannot live by this creed for even five minutes.

As an epistemology, nihilism has the same problem that relativism has. To say that there is no truth is to make a truth claim. Perhaps our three-word retort to such a claim might be "Is that so?" If it is not so that there is no truth, then the nihilist must cease to be a nihilist. And if it is so that there is no truth, then it is true that there is no truth, and the argument is refuted again.

The two dilemmas of the nihilist join together once more in the truth that those who deny that there is truth not only affirm that there is truth, but seek to persuade us of their view. But if there is no objective standard of right and wrong, then there is no reason to try persuading others of that truth. It is not wrong to believe that there is a standard, and it is not right to make the case that there is no standard. If there is no standard of truth, then there is no truth to seek to persuade people of by writing books and essays. When Nietzsche sat down to write *Thus Spake Zarathustra*, he was, by writing the book, denying the very contents of it. When Camus wrote *The Myth of Sisyphus*, he was engaged in a fruitless, Sisyphean ordeal of making his case that cases cannot be made. When Sartre sat down to write the play *No Exit*, he was boxed in by his own internal inconsistencies. And when earnest young men and women read these works and are convinced by them, they are denying the truth of what they have read. Truth is then better than falsehood to those who say there is no truth. And right is better than wrong to those who deny there is a right and a wrong. Without courage, and perhaps even with it, any of us would rightly go mad trying to affirm what we are denying, and denying what we are affirming.

For all their willingness to look at the hard truth of meaninglessness, there is a fundamental lack of honesty among nihilists. They do not, and will not, live what they affirm and what they deny. In fact, were a modern-day Diogenes to take his lantern and go out in search of an honest nihilist, his search might look something like this:

I understand now why I was having such a hard time. Hunting big game, while dangerous and challenging, at least has this as an advantage: it is rather hard to miss a water buffalo. However, I was hunting small game, armed not with a rifle, but with my trusty lantern. My name is Diogenes, and I seek nothing. Well, not nothing. Actually, I'm looking for something far rarer still, an honest nihilist, one who truly believes in no truth, one whose heartfelt goal is to eschew the pursuit of all goals. Down the cobbled streets I roamed, until my lantern caught a strange shadow. It was a man, or rather, what was left of one.

"Pardon me, good sir, would you mind telling me your name?" I asked with all innocence.

"Why do you call me good?" the stranger asked. "Nothing and no one and nowhere is good. My name is Nyetski." Perhaps, already, my search was at an end.

"Do you mind if I ask you a few questions?"

"It is all the same to me," Nyetski replied.

"Can you please tell me what drove you to write all those books, those essays, to teach all those courses? What exactly was your goal in bravely proclaiming your message of nothing?"

"It is of the utmost importance that the people of the world come to understand the truth of nihilism. They must learn that there is no truth, no goodness, no beauty, no reason for being. My one goal was to set people free, so that they might do the brave and right and true thing that I have done, and embrace the nothing."

"Uh, I'm not sure I follow you, sir. Would it be fair to say that your goal was to persuade others of the truth that there is no truth and no goal?"

"You are trying to trap me, strange man with a lantern. But I am too wise for you. I know this is nonsense. I love and embrace the nonsense; that is my very point. I am the one who bravely faced the nonsense, and who taught others to do the same."

"Why? Why not face the nonsense like a coward? Why not be a part of the herd? Is it wrong to be in the herd that affirms that there is wrong, and right to be the master who denies that there is right? Why not flee the nonsense like a cringing sissy? Face this, Nyetski, if you have the courage: you are a fraud."

"Wait!" shouted Nyetski.

"Why should I?" I called over my shoulder as I headed off. My search took me over borders and centuries. Rumor had it that there was a whole gaggle of nihilists to be found congregating in France in the 1940s. I found my way to an out-of-the-way café in Paris.

"Have a seat, stranger," one of the patrons offered.

I explained my quest: "I'm in search of nihilists. Do you gentleman know of any?"

"*Oui, oui, mon frère,* your labors have not been fruitless, for you have come to the right place. I am Canyou. Welcome to our little café. I would suggest, however, that you not eat the food. It might give you some nausea."

"Hey, man, don't have the cow," the other interrupted. "Just a while ago it was crawling with flies. I'm Bartre. Who are you?"

"My name is Diogenes, and I'm in search of a sincere and honest nihilist."

"That's us, man, we're heavy into nothing, sincerely. Why, between the two of us, we've written plays and novels, poems and books, all trying to get the word out about nothing. We're the greatest fans of nothing you'll ever find. Of course, things have been kind of slow for us of late, what with the Nazis occupying Paris. We've been so busy risking our necks in the underground, that we just have no time for nothing anymore."

"But please, can't you see?" I implored. "You can't have it both ways. Why write? Why fight? Why do anything, when there's no reason? What's the purpose when you say there is no purpose?"

"You don't get it, Di, my friend. It's because there's no reason that we can do things for no reason."

"There you go again, trying to justify, trying to make reasonable, your claim to have no reason, trying to make sense of acting without sense. Why, the two of you are no better than that old faker Nyetski."

"You knew Nyetski? Oh, we love him. He was the greatest, all that courage in facing up to no goodness. Why, it positively breaks our heart that we never really got to know the man. He was super. It's so sad that he died."

I paid for my drink and made off, without trying to explain again to the rebels without a cause that without a cause they could not rebel. To argue further was as pointless as they were. My search, however, was far from over. Imbued with a new sense of purpose, I set off in search of purposelessness. I visited still more cafés, beatnik bars, hippie communes. Everywhere I found something, exactly what I wasn't looking for. The beatniks seemed to show promise, embracing the religion of nothing, becoming dharma bums. Why did they do it? Sadly, they never did it for nothing. Instead, they were always in search of something: peace, or nirvana, or some perceived good, even if that good thing was on the other side of the doors of perception. The purest of them were guilty of the crimes of their fathers, zealously spreading their religion of nothingness. I lugged my lantern through New York's Central Park, discouraged and dejected. Nothing, it seemed, was nowhere to be found. I sat down beside an old statue and leaned back. But wait. This was some strange statue. It had a certain warmth, a definite softness.

"Excuse me," I cried out. "I had no idea you were a live person. You were just sitting so still that I took you to be a statue. I guess I must be overly tired. Will you forgive me?" The man gave no reply. "You see, I've been on a sort of quest. It has taken me all over the world and all through time. I've been shining my lantern through the streets of history, searching for an honest nihilist. Do you know what an honest nihilist is?" He still did not answer.

"They believe—at least they claim to believe—that there is no truth, no goodness, no reason for being or for doing. But so far every last one of them has been a hypocrite. Don't you just hate hypocrites?" His face betrayed no emotion. "Sorry, I'm blathering on and on about my troubles. I haven't given you a chance to get a word in edgewise. What is your story? Why are you out here in the park sitting so still?" Still he sat. "Is something the matter? Are you mute? Can you give me some sign? I speak many languages."

The longer he sat, devoid of emotion, the more my emotions swelled. "Say, friend, would you mind terribly if I were to cart you off somewhere?" Still nothing.

My search is over now. I've bagged my trophy, the world's only sincere nihilist. He hasn't changed a bit since I brought him home. I just propped him up on my mantle, and there he sits to this day. I didn't even have to hire a taxidermist. I did, however, put a little sign underneath him, so he would not frighten my guests. It reads, "Here is Bartleby, the world's only honest nihilist. Don't be fooled by foolish imitations."

Nihilism—indeed, any system that denies the possibility of knowing any sort of transcendent teleology, or purpose—must lead to catatonia, that psychological state in which a person sits motionless or lies like a stone slab, not eating, smiling, or doing anything. Our choices are made in the service of higher ends or goals. We do what we do in order to do something bigger. I'm writing this today because I'd like to get this book done by my deadline. I'd like to get it done so that it might have all the support and time it needs at the publishers. I want that to be done so that more people will read it, and, God willing, be helped by it. And it is my hope that, as people are helped by it, God will be glorified. That is the end of my ends, indeed my chief end. And it drives all the ends that lead to it. One cannot cut off the final end and still make sense of any other end.

That, however, is precisely what professing nihilists pretend to do. To point out to them the utter inconsistency of their words and actions will not often cause them to abandon one or the other. In the nihilist system, because it rejects reason as an arbiter of truth, because it embraces hypocrisy as no more wicked than sincerity, there is neither guilt nor shame. This is the system that is the end of all systems. In the old modernist world, if we could demonstrate that a particular proposition or system of thought was necessarily absurd, those who held that view would concede that it therefore could not be true. When we engaged our opponents in debate, even when they failed to recognize the God of the universe as the source of all truth, they recognized that there was a truth, and that irrationality was the hallmark of falsehood. With the nihilist, however, irrationality is not only not feared, but embraced. There are real flesh-and-blood people who profess to hold these views, and we are called to proclaim the gospel to them. How can we tear down this stronghold, so that those who have locked themselves in it might come to embrace the gospel?

We can certainly pray that the nihilist who boasts in public about the irrationality of his view is internally troubled by that irrationality. We can continue to push that irrationality more and more into view for the nihilist. When

he boldly asserts, "I've embraced the irrational system of nihilism," we can shout for joy, shake his hand, slap him on
the back, and respond, "I'm delighted to hear, my new
brother, that you have embraced the Christian faith." If
there is no standard of truth, then it is just as true that he
is a Christian as it is true that he is a nihilist. If someone
says he is a nihilist, he has no standard by which to object
to being considered a Christian. Or perhaps we can press
him on the moral issues that he cares about. If there is no
standard of truth, "I am a nihilist" can mean "I believe in
slavery, the subjugation of women, the wanton destruction
of the environment, the torture of animals, and that nihilists deserve to have their worldly goods taken from them
and to be subjected to the most painful and humiliating
death imaginable." Even the most seared conscience has its
limits, and it usually starts with one's own nose. That is, the
nihilist may wish to be free of all morality, to exhibit the
master morality, but he probably doesn't want to have a
master over him who has no sense of morality. In short, we
can continue to press on the nihilists the implications of
their view. And if they still want to live in a world of absurdity, there may come a time when we have to follow the
troubling injunction of Christ himself, and shake the dust
off our feet as we walk away.

## CHAPTER NINE

# TRANSCENDING THE IMMANENT

I have heard it said, though I do not remember where, that the definition of insanity is "repeating the same behavior over and over and expecting different re-sults." If that is true, and if we have made our case against all the epistemologies posited by the world, then it would appear that we live in a mad, mad, mad, mad, mad world. But we should not be surprised. Scripture gives us fore-warning when it says, "The fool has said in his heart, 'There is no God'" (Ps. 14:1). God calls such people fools. We too would be utterly foolish and inconsistent if we claimed to believe that the Bible is the Word of God, our only rule of faith and practice, and then resisted the idea that those who deny God are fools. If we believe the Bible, we must accept that those who do not believe the Bible are not only in error, not only in danger, but in the bonds of foolishness.

Whether they are philosophers, scientists, psycholo-

gists, or ordinary people, each of them has pursued a goal.
Like Diogenes, they have taken their lantern and set out on
a quest. What are they looking for? What is the appeal of
this road that leads only into a ditch? People are actually
searching for two things, two mutually exclusive things,
which explains why they keep making shipwreck of their
minds. Our foolish friends and neighbors are trying at the
same time to save the phenomena and save themselves
from the wrath of God, or at least escape from the knowledge that his wrath is coming.

"Saving the phenomena" has always been the goal of
the scientist, a central element of the scientific method.
The scientist begins his work by carefully observing the
phenomena. By "phenomena" we mean little bits of information. Newton sits beneath a tree and watches as first one
and then another apple falls to the ground. He notes these
phenomena. Over to his left there is perhaps another tree,
with no apples, but he notices the leaves beginning to fall
from the tree. First they are set loose from the branch, and
then they descend to the earth. He writes all these discreet
events down in his notebook. He has made a series of empirical observations. His next step is to see if he can come
up with a hypothesis that will explain, or "save," the phenomena. The hypothesis must explain why each of the
recorded events happened as it did. Next, he must come up
with a means of testing the hypothesis. What experiment
will show whether the hypothesis is true or false? If the test
validates the hypothesis, it might then become a theory.
But suppose the hypothesis runs something like this: There
is a force in the universe that draws all red things toward

the center of the earth. The red apples fall from the tree because of that force, but the green ones remain on the tree.
With this hypothesis, I have saved the phenomena, explaining things in a way that makes sense of what I've seen
and leaves no anomalies. And my hypothesis seems to be
confirmed when I observe, on a second tree, that the green
leaves stay up on the tree. And when autumn comes along,
and the leaves change, the red ones fall to the ground. The
trouble with the theory is that it fails to explain the falling
yellow leaves of another tree. I can't quickly add "Yellow
things also fall to the center of the earth" to my hypothesis,
because that would leave a rather large anomaly in the
sky—the sun.

So when we try to save the phenomena, we try to
come up with an explanation for all the things that we observe. For our purposes, though, we need to understand the
idea a little more broadly. The pagan wants to have an understanding of the world in which it makes sense. He does
not want to end up in foolishness or insanity. Because he
still has the image of God in him, despite the devastating
effects of the Fall, he wants some knowledge of what is true,
of what is good, and of his own end or purpose. At the very
least, the unbeliever is eager not to be abused or destroyed
by other unbelievers. One of his goals is to understand the
world in such a way that it is not good or right for him to
be destroyed.

On the other hand, the unbeliever has a second, often
more powerful drive: to avoid God. The unbeliever (and
unbelieving culture at large) wants to see the phenomena
of the world reasonably explained, but without a God who

will one day judge him. This is an important part of what the apostle Paul is talking about when he explains the universal guilt of mankind:

> For the wrath of God is revealed from heaven against all ungodliness and unrighteousness of men, who suppress the truth in unrighteousness, because what may be known of God is manifest in them, for God has shown it to them. For since the creation of the world His invisible attributes are clearly seen, being understood by the things that are made, even His eternal power and Godhead, so that they are without excuse, because, although they knew God, they did not glorify Him as God, nor were thankful, but became futile in their thoughts, and their foolish hearts were darkened. Professing to be wise, they became fools, and changed the glory of the incorruptible God into an image made like corruptible man—and birds and four-footed beasts and creeping things. (Rom. 1:18–23)

To be thankful is to recognize dependence, which in turn brings with it obligation.

Historically, the most common way to make sense of the world, but to be free from divine wrath, has been to posit a God (or gods) who either could be easily appeased or had no wrath to appease. This has been the method of choice for all the systems that we have considered in this book. Instead of merely constructing new gods out of creatures, they have constructed entire worldviews out of the creation. Their entire systems are bound to this world, that is, utterly immanent. Their systems of knowledge never get beyond this material world—whether it be some variety of empiricism, where only our senses can show us truth; or some variety of determinism, such as naturalism, which says that our convictions are only chemical reactions, or behaviorism, which says that our convictions are determined by our environment. These systems all end in man, the creature.

All of these systems promise the great reward of human autonomy or self-rule. In these systems, there is no standard of truth or morality above me, and therefore I am immune to judgment. I become a law unto myself. All those who pronounce judgment against me are also stuck in this autonomous, closed system, so closed that their pronouncements cannot touch me. (This again highlights the problem with relativism, whether the more happy version or the darker nihilist variety: In order for it to work, relativism must be absolute. It's no good for morality to be relative to me, if it is really objective and I will one day be judged by that objective standard.) Rather than trying to make sense of the universe, I only want to construct a universe in which I am okay and can do as I please. To save the phenomena in my worldview, I am willing to borrow from another worldview. Thus, the behaviorist borrows the truth that we are rational creatures, and then proceeds to make a rational argument that we are irrational creatures whose views are formed only by our environment. Similarly, the logical positivist, while affirming that only those ideas that can be empirically verified have any meaning, ascribes meaning to his empirically unverifiable thesis. And the nihilist, while denying that there are such things as right and wrong, deems it wrong to believe in any worldview other than nihilism, and right to teach that there is no right. To put it plainly, these people are using Christian truth, while denying that Christianity has any truth. They are not standing on sandy ground, but, as Francis Schaeffer once put it, with both feet planted firmly in midair.

Without a transcendent standard, we are left with the motto of the first self-conscious humanist, the Greek philosopher Heraclitus, who coined the phrase *homo mensura,* "man the measure." On this view, man, the creature, is the highest standard for answering all of our ultimate questions. The difficulty is that the universe is not populated by man, but by men. Men have a tendency to disagree. There is no man who is the measure, just men, each of whom seeks to be the measure. Consider an example from recent history. Our nation, in the 2000 election, received not only a lesson in political science, but a lesson in epistemology. One party went from court to court, trying to get a judge to order a recount of the presidential ballots that registered no vote with the counting machines. We were treated to images of vote counters holding ballots up to the light to figure out the voters' intent. Chad became our daily companion, as we wondered if he was pregnant, and if so, what that meant. The Republicans argued, ultimately successfully, that such a recount was biased, because there was no uniform standard by which intent could be determined. How deep is a dimple? How many threads may Chad hold onto and still make it into the vote count? We had witnesses watching the count—one a Republican, one a Democrat, and one an election official. Those officials would settle any disagreement about the voter's intent, and with so much at stake, one can be assured that the two witnesses representing the two parties often disagreed. For all intents and purposes, then, the election official would make the call, and probably on the basis of his own political leanings.

That is essentially how we as a culture decide moral and epistemological questions—by counting noses. Now it is not man who is the measure, but the majority of men. This is supposed to be the glory of democracy. One wag, however, rightly described democracy as two wolves and one lamb deciding what was for dinner. When there is no transcendent standard and men disagree, the one with greater power will determine what is right. In the end, under all these systems, might makes right. This is precisely how the debate over abortion is handled in our country. When we discuss whether or not a woman ought to have a legal right to destroy her unborn child, those in favor argue that a woman has a right to choose. But where, precisely, does that right come from? Few, if any, would argue that the God of the universe has determined that a woman has such a right. Most argue over *Roe v. Wade* by appealing to *Roe v. Wade*, by begging the question. A woman ought to have the right to choose because she has the right to choose. The highest standard for determining right and wrong becomes for us the Supreme Court.

Whenever truth or morality is determined by majority vote, we degenerate into some form of statism. Statism is much more than a large, intrusive government. As an ism, it speaks of the apotheosis of the state, the making of the state into a god. It is not a mere inconvenience; it is idolatry. It should not surprise us that in many cultures around the world and throughout history, the state or its symbols have been worshiped. Nor should we think that we are too sophisticated for such things. Philosophy, like nature, abhors a vacuum. When we will not have God in our thinking, when he is banished as the highest good, it will always be men, or their collective form, the state, that will fill that void. Whether the state deems it right to allow the killing of unborn children, or takes it upon itself to kill its real or perceived enemies, if there is no higher authority to which to appeal, then it becomes tyrannical. If the state is the final authority, there is no appeal against "the final solution." If there are only men, there is no moral standard that can keep some men from killing others.

When the state is deemed to be the final arbiter in all things epistemological or moral, when it exercises sovereign authority, it begins to see itself, as its subjects begin to see it, as having sovereign ability. We do not merely ask the state what it is we are to do, we ask the state to make things right. We ask the state to remake the reality that we don't like, to repeal God's very laws of nature. Consider what has happened in the space of less than a century. Early in the twentieth century, the nation experienced an epidemic of influenza. Thousands of people caught the disease and soon died. The nation, in general, responded to this calamity by getting on its knees and beseeching God for deliverance. We prayed, and God heard our prayers, and the epidemic mercifully came to an end. We had a calamity that was bigger than us, and so we turned to something bigger than us to end it. Fast forward to the mid-1980s. There is a new epidemic that is killing tens of thousands of people: AIDS. How did the nation respond this time? Again, the nation, in general, got on its knees and pleaded for deliverance from this dreadful killer. But this time the god to whom the prayers were directed was the federal government. We screamed and we clamored for the government to do something, to make the disease stop. If they are the arbiters of reality, then let them make a reality with no more AIDS. Washington has responded by doing the only thing it knows how to do: tax and spend. The state has to be our god, because we do not want God to be our god.

The epistemological vacuum that was left when we banished God from our thinking about thinking has been filled by the state. It tells us, albeit by counting the noses of its citizens, what we are to think. The moral vacuum that was left when we banished God from our thinking has been filled by the state. It tells us that what is legal is right, and what is illegal is wrong. The next thing to go is our teleology. Without a transcendent teleology, something else will have to tell us what our purpose is. Soon in the West it will clearly be the state that fills the teleological vacuum, that not only provides the answer, but is the answer. Soon we will be told to consider not what our new god can do for us, but what we can do for our new god. For now, we have scattered and fragmented substitutes for the God of the universe: social causes, saving the environment, ending discrimination, seeking harmonic convergence.

We are not the first to find ourselves in this boat. Nor

am I the first to point out that once the transcendent is taken out of the picture, it is impossible to have a real and lasting ultimate teleology or purpose for all that we do in our lives. In fact, one who is far wiser than me, whose name is synonymous with wisdom, belabored this very point for us around three thousand years ago. Solomon begins his great philosophical and literary work, Ecclesiastes, not at the philosophical beginning of despair, but in the very heart of it. He begins with, "The words of the Preacher, the son of David, king in Jerusalem. 'Vanity of vanities,' says the Preacher; 'vanity of vanities, all is vanity' " (1:1–2). This is no chipper beginning to a piece of literature. This is not the kind of light reading that we take to the beach. Solomon, the son of David, is telling us that there is no teleology, that none of our purposes can stand, that every-thing is vain and pointless. This is not, however, the con-viction of Solomon. Rather, the book is written as an extended exposition of the fruit of looking at the world from the perspective of being "under the sun." That ex-pression appears again and again in this work. It is a poetic way of denying the transcendent. If there is no transcen-dent purpose, then all the things we strive for are merely striving after the wind. Chapter after chapter of Ecclesiastes consists of Solomon cataloguing for us many of the things that men tend to hold as their *summum bonum*, their "high-est good," the end for which their lives are lived.

This book of wisdom, ironically, begins by showing the vanity of pursuing wisdom under the sun. Solomon was an expert on wisdom. He sought it truly beyond the sun, where God was pleased to grant it to him. Under the sun, however, it brings only sorrow and grief. The Preacher begins where unbelieving philosophy ends, with sorrow and a recognition that it is nothing but folly.

Solomon next turns his attention to pleasure, taking the route of the hedonist. But here, too, he runs into a dead end. "I said of laughter, 'It is madness'; and of mirth, 'What does it accomplish?' " (2:2). It makes no sense, either, if there is nothing beyond the sun. It is no better than pain, if there is no transcendent standard by which to judge. And it ends in death, sooner or later.

Finding wisdom and pleasure unable to provide an abiding purpose under the sun, Solomon sets his mind to achieve great things. He sets about to build great buildings and plant vineyards, orchards, and gardens. He begins to build up his household, acquiring male and female servants, herds and flocks. He accumulates great wealth in gold and silver. "And indeed all was vanity and grasping for the wind. There was no profit under the sun" (2:11).

This last attempt may best describe the lives of quiet desperation lived by too many in our consumerist age. Our teleology is given no thought, but becomes by default the pursuit of personal peace and affluence. We suppress not only our God-given knowledge of God, but also the knowledge that there is an end to our lives. We seek to avoid the foolishness of the happy humanists by refusing to remember that we will return to the dust. It is, however, the nature of the problem that precludes the solution. To get away from the judgment of God, we must get away from the transcendent. And once we have cut ourselves off from the transcendent, once we look at our life from a perspective under the sun, there is no way to discover a transcendent purpose for our life, a purpose that will not only live on after our death, but make sense of our life here and now.

Our life, however, is not lived under the sun, but under the Son. In Christ there is not an end, but the end. Our chief end is clear, that we are to glorify God and enjoy him forever. Our escape from the wrath of God is secure in the life, death, resurrection, and ascension of Jesus Christ. We have peace and purpose. Outside of Christ, however, one cannot have both.

## PART THREE

# AFTER DARKNESS, LIGHT

## CHAPTER TEN

# I GOTTA BE ME

'm sure it was a truth he didn't like to think about too often, but it was true nonetheless—he was a cliché. It's bad enough to be a cliché, but worse to be a clichéd cliché fighter. That's what Roy Kauffman was. I imagine that most college campuses have at least one guy like him, the local guru, the Svengali. At Grove City College, where I studied literature and philosophy, Roy was the guy. He was an English professor, and if you wanted to be in his class, you had to sign up early. Virtually every performance was sold out.

Grove City was rather an odd college when I was there. Both the faculty and the student body were strongly mixed. Many students were there because it was a small and comfortable Christian college. The Christian part wasn't in name only. A sizable percentage of students would enter the cafeteria for Sunday lunch still dressed for church. (And a few even dressed for lunch to make it look like they had been to church. Grove City was a place where, through hypocrisy, vice paid homage to virtue.) Grove City also had a reputation for providing a quality education at a bargain price. And so there were many students there who had no interest in Christianity.

The faculty was also mixed. Once one got to know the professors, one could safely guess under which president they had been hired. There were devoted Christians teaching there, as well as others who were devoted to undermining it. Roy Kauffman was the best of the latter group. He was tender to the disaffected youth who rebelled against the church. And he delighted to puncture the comparative innocence of the typical Christian students in his class. It seemed that no class was complete until he had made some sweet sorority sister cry.

Dr. Kauffman graded us on the basis of journals in which we were to interact with the novels we read for his class. It was common knowledge that if one demonstrated a knowledge of the books and bared one's soul in one's journal, a good grade was a certainty. Attendance in the class was utterly unnecessary. That's what appealed to me.

It took me a while, however, to learn that little trick of the college student trade. It was early in my career when I first crossed swords with the underdog's hero. Dr. Kauffman was in the midst of a typical paean to skepticism, arguing from the objective reality that we often disagree about what objective reality is that there is no objective reality. He was in rare form, using his charm and William Faulkner's novel As I Lay Dying to the fullest effect. He reached a climax in much the same way that Pontius Pilate did, asking, "What is truth?" At this point, we were sup-

posed to be dumbfounded by his profundity. We were supposed to cower before such a display of courage. We were
supposed to imbibe of his skepticism and then thank him
for it. I raised my hand. He looked at me, surprised. What
was this pup doing, interrupting his performance?

"Yes, young man?" he said.

"What is," I replied.

Well, Dr. Kauffman soon regained his composure and
his confidence in the truth of his skepticism. He knew one
thing for certain, it would not take long to dispose of me
and my belief in certainty.

"Can you, young man, perhaps give us an example of
what is?"

"I am."

Now, I was neither affirming God as an example of
what is (by referring to the Hebrew name Yahweh, which
can be translated "I am that I am"), nor suggesting that I
was in the process of giving an example of what is. Rather,
"I am" was the truth that I was affirming. I was standing my
ground on my own existence, using it to demonstrate not
only that there is a reality, but that that reality is knowable.
I was calling up the ghost of René Descartes in my defense
against this skeptic.

Descartes might have, at one time, delighted to join
Dr. Kauffman in his skepticism. Descartes's goal was certainty. He has been called the father of modern philosophy.
His work came at a time of great cultural unrest. Skepticism
was on the rise. The sciences were in a muddle, thanks to
the work of Kepler, Galileo, and others. Religion was no
longer a steady and stable force in Western culture, as the

Reformation had come and created controversy and discord. One could no longer look to Rome for definitive answers. Descartes's genius was that he tried to get to certainty through uncertainty. He decided that in order for him to discover whether or not anything was truly knowable, he would have to begin by doubting everything. He refused to take anything for granted. If an idea came with any doubts, it had to be discarded. He was looking for the indubitable truth or truths on which he could hang his hat. He wanted to be certain that he would never be accused of credulity. He wasn't going to challenge the assumptions, but banish them. He would exclude all empirical input, and see what he could see. And what he saw was that he had to be.

Descartes is remembered for that little Latin nugget, *Cogito ergo sum*, "I think, therefore I am." It was actually one step removed from where he started, which might have been *Dubito ergo sum*, "I doubt, therefore I am." In his zeal not to take anything for granted, not to allow an untested or unproved idea to inhabit his mind, Descartes realized that there had to be a mind in the first place. Perhaps his thinking went something like this: I doubt the existence of the external world, because I doubt the reliability of my senses. That outside world could be a phantom, a nasty trick played on me by some nasty deity. I doubt that I even exist. Wait a minute. Who doubts that he exists? In order to doubt that one exists, one would first have to be. One can surely doubt the existence of others, but one cannot doubt one's own existence. One would have to be and not be at the same time and in the same relationship. One can doubt any number of things, but one cannot doubt oneself away. The most radical skeptic must not only assert the truth that there is no truth, but must assert the truth that it is he who is asserting that there is no truth.

Dr. Kauffman tried to confuse the matter by questioning my existence. "How can I know that you exist?" he asked. "That's something of a long walk," I answered, "but I know that you cannot deny that you exist. That is truth." It was he this time, I believe, who was saved by the bell.

If the claim is made that there is no knowable truth, that claim can be discarded as invalid by demonstrating the existence of only one truth. And since that claim is a truth claim, it carries with it not only the seeds of its own destruction, but the full-grown tree. That first truth claim implies a second truth claim, and a third one. There is the necessary claim that the claimant is the one making the claim. That is, when the nihilist says there is no truth, he is also saying, "I believe there is no truth." And, as Descartes reminds us, there is the claim by the claimant that he exists. I must be, in order to be one who believes there is no truth.

We may be piling on the skeptics here, as we have already shown that we should be skeptical of their skepticism. But we must now move on to the next stage in our apologetical battles. We have done our negative negative apologetics, dealing with the truth claims, or truth denials, of our opponents, and shown them to be false. However, we have not done the more difficult work of establishing the truthfulness of our own worldview. We should not be satisfied with a tie, with merely showing that the other view is

wrong. We still have to demonstrate what a sound epistemology looks like. Is there a legitimate way to distinguish
truth from falsehood? And if there is, where do we start?

Here we encounter what I call the epistemic dilemma.
In dealing with the competing epistemologies that the
world has to offer, we have tried to get at them by attacking their foundations, by testing their fundamental assumptions against themselves. But there will always be a problem
with any epistemological foundation, principally, that it
cannot be proved. There can be no foundation under our
foundation. Or, to put it another way, we have no tools
with which to make our first tools. If there is a foundation
beneath our foundation, what foundation is below that
lower foundation? If we have tools with which we make our
tools, then where are the tools to make those tools? Our
goal is not at all unlike the goal of Descartes, to reach epistemological bedrock.

Consider the subject of geometry. I wasn't such a sassy
student in geometry class. It was a struggle for me. Geometry seeks to discover or to demonstrate particular truths
about particular shapes. It does so through the application
of a series of rules or theorems, most of which also at some
point have to be demonstrated. But geometry has the same
problem. It must start with something, and cannot start before it starts. Geometry begins with the raw, unsupported
supposition of the point, the line, and the plane. There are
no theorems that prove what a point is. Instead, the first
geometric theorems are built out of the supposition of the
point, the line, and the plane. These are the foundations,
or the tools, that make all the laws of geometry possible.

In the next few chapters, we are going to consider a series of unprovable, but nevertheless indispensable starting points, such that there might be knowledge. Our dilemma will remain. Despite being unable to prove the truthfulness of these foundational rules for knowing, however, I will demonstrate that they cannot be denied, and that, in fact, to deny them is to affirm them. They are inescapable.

Some suggest that our given, our starting point, must be God himself. It is certainly true in one sense that God is our starting point. After all, once there was God and nothing else. We are the work of his hands. Without him, there would be no us. He is our ontological beginning, indeed, the ontological beginning of all other things. He alone has the power of being, and it is in him that we live and move and have our being. This does not mean, however, that knowing him is the beginning of our knowing. Our knowing begins not with him, but with ourselves. One more caveat. That our knowing begins with ourselves does not mean that we have a higher degree of certitude about ourselves than we do about God's existence. We need not move at all times from more certainty to less, but can move from absolute certainty to absolute certainty. Nor am I suggesting that we know about our existence before (in a temporal sense) we know about God's existence. We know both from our beginning, for God has revealed himself to all. As Paul tells us, those outside his grace deny the knowledge that they already have. Those who would deny God, or would seek to substitute a creature for him, do so not because they do not know God, but because they do not want to acknowledge what they already know. In a later chapter, we will see if we can move from our initial nonnegotiables to the existence of God, to make those who deny what they know either concede or recognize that their professed views are foolish.

There are those who argue that God is not only the beginning of our being, but the beginning of our knowing. The dominant view in Reformed circles, known as presuppositionalism, argues that we must begin our pursuit of knowledge by presupposing God, that any other starting point is bound to end in absurdity. The difficulty with this view, although it has much that is attractive about it, is that we cannot, in this sense, begin with God. The reason why brings us back to Descartes. We all begin our knowing with ourselves, because it is we who are doing the knowing. To those who say, "I begin with God" or "I presuppose God," we ask, "*Who* begins with God?" One might try to get around this problem with a semantic trick, and affirm instead, "God is." While it is certainly true that God is, and that his being is in no way dependent upon our acknowledgment of it, we nevertheless ask, "Says who?" We do not start with God, but with ourselves.

The good news is that as we consider these nonnegotiables for knowledge, we see that, like self-consciousness, our presuppositional friends actually do start exactly where we start. They just don't want to admit it. To start at the beginning is inescapable. We will also see that our presuppositional friends, having started there, actually make an outstanding, indeed compelling case for the existence of God.

Descartes has shown that it is perfectly safe to start with oneself. For, once again, to deny our existence is to affirm our existence. In the strange history of philosophy, there have been those who would deny the truth of Descartes and try to deny their own existence. There are two ways to deal with this radical skepticism, one philosophical, the other practical. The more practical way to deal with them is simply to let them do it. One need not debate an opponent who refuses to show up. Grant their premise, that they do not exist, and then get on with the business of life, with one less obstacle in the way. We are doing those who deny their existence no favor by taking their argument seriously, for the more carefully we listen to them, the more we must affirm that they exist. It would seem that the kind thing to do would be to ignore anyone who would go to this extreme in order to avoid considering the wrath of God.

The more philosophical approach is once again to attack the premise with the premise. To the person who claims, "I do not exist," we offer this refutation: "Who does not exist?" The existence of "I" in "I do not exist" contradicts the words "do not exist" in "I do not exist." It's that simple. The claim contains its own refutation.

But some still persist, and equivocate on either the nature of the self or the nature of existence. Some people, when they say "I do not exist," take the view that they may not be flesh-and-blood people, occupying time and space, but only a figment of our imagination. But if they are a figment of our imagination, they still have a form of existence. "I" may not be a person, but it is still a figment. The figment has to exist, and the person experiencing the figment has to exist, at least in some form. Even if the whole created order is but a sort of ruse, if we are all merely play-ers on some madman's stage, we still would not and could not signify nothing. We would still be players, and there would still be a stage. Pick any metaphysic you want, and you will still be you doing the picking.

Whether we are seeking to honor God, as presupposi-tionalists do, or are seeking to avoid him, as some have done, by denying that we start with ourselves we are at the same time affirming that we start with ourselves. It is where we start, unavoidably. We cannot prove our own existence, for we have to assume it in order even to try. If we fail to as-sume our existence, we have no "we" with which to try to conclude it. But we can see that we cannot deny our own existence. To deny it is to affirm it.

This may seem like much ado about not very much. Why bother spending time seeking to demonstrate some-thing as universally recognized as our existence? Philoso-phers can sometimes go through all manner of mental contortions and gyrations to reach conclusions that are as plain as day. Of course we exist, and only a fool would deny it. We belabor this point for two important reasons. First, there are fools out there who do deny their existence, and it is important that we give them an answer. We know that they exist, and if we want them to escape from the wrath of God, then we had better help them understand the fool-ishness of their position. Second, we are trying to get down to brass tacks, to start out with the very basics of how we know things. It is only natural that it would seem simple at first. Foundations are not usually terribly sophisticated. The important thing is that they be sturdy.

As helpful as Descartes is in helping us to understand the necessity of our own existence, he did not, of course, create us or give us the certainty of our existence. People knew that they existed long before Descartes said so, and for the same reasons that we have listed. No doubt Adam, without sin, had no reason to try to hide from the obvious and recognized his own existence. And men have known it ever since, even those who have claimed to deny it.

You may recall that we earlier described positive negative apologetics as the answering of objections to our position. We were neither arguing against other views nor making our own case, but answering objections to our view. Here again we have as our advantage the fact that our opponent cannot deny our position without first assuming it. While I have a great interest in the field of apologetics, even I would not waste my time trying to convince a pink-striped zebra that he didn't exist. Nor would I try to persuade my dear wife that she doesn't exist. There is no reason to try to persuade anyone that he doesn't exist. If he does exist, I would be in error. If he doesn't exist, I would be wasting my time.

This is what we are reduced to sometimes in dealing with unbelief. Some people, in order to escape their knowledge of the wrath of God, will sacrifice much of what they know, including their own existence. They will deny the obvious in order to escape the obvious. If I exist, they recognize, I must answer to my Creator. I cannot deny my Creator and still affirm my existence, and so I will deny my existence. These sad people need to recognize that they do exist, and that they know that they exist, and that God exists, and that they know that he exists, and that the only way to escape his wrath is to embrace his Son. Perhaps we can help them along the way by beginning where they begin, by starting with the truth of their own existence. And perhaps, as we do so, the Spirit who graciously gave them the life they want to deny, will graciously give them a new life that cannot be denied. While we begin with ourselves, recognizing our own existence, that is the happy ending we are always working toward as we do the work of apologetics.

## CHAPTER ELEVEN

# TO BE OR NOT TO BE

I was something of a slow learner. While my father's words of wisdom helped me to break away from the whole angry young man routine that I went through in high school, there was one vestige that remained. I wiped the scowl off my face, but kept my hair long. The next time I saw my father, after his gentle chastening on cynicism, he was not very gentle. I was home from school on a holiday break. I flew into the local airport and was greeted by hugs from both of my parents. We retrieved my bags, made our way to the family car, and proceeded down the highway toward home. My father is usually a maddeningly cautious driver. But not this time. He would look in the rearview mirror, and then step down heavily on the gas pedal. Finally, between clenched teeth he said to my mother, "We need to stop at a barber and do something about his hair." She reasoned that it could wait until I got to my regular barber. He didn't want to wait, and he didn't wait any further to let me know how unhappy he was about my hair. He wanted to know what the big idea was; he told me that he knew that I had grown my hair long for the express purpose of aggravating him, that my hair was a slap in his face. He gave an eloquent and passionate discourse on all the hateful and disrespectful reasons I had for growing my hair. I let him finish, but only because I had no other choice.

"Dad," I said with some trepidation, "none of what you just said has anything to do with why I grew my hair long. I was not doing it to hurt you, for I have no desire to hurt you. You are assuming that all people who have long hair fit in the category of those whom you knew back in the sixties who had long hair. I've not joined some anachronistic sixties subculture. I'm not out drinking or using drugs. I haven't joined a rock band, nor am I spending my days protesting a war that ended a decade ago. You are making completely unwarranted assumptions in your reasoning about my hair."

One might think that that would have settled the matter. I was feeling pretty good about myself. I had kept my cool, affirmed my respect for my father, and certainly made peace. Surely the conversation could now end.

"Son, while I agree that you may believe it, I don't believe a word of what you just said. But if I'm wrong about your reasons, why don't you go ahead and tell me your reasons for doing this?"

"Well, I guess it's because"—now this was, and is, embarrassing—"because I don't want people to think that I'm just ordinary. I don't want to be this boring high school kid who is only interested in girls and cars and clothes and stupid stuff like that."

Now, having embarrassed me, my father was willing to be a little more gracious as he gave me a verbal scalping. "That may be an admirable goal, son, but you need to understand that people will see that hair and not reach that conclusion about you. They will see you as rebellious. They will not think you're filled with zeal, but with hatred for the things that matter. They will think all you care about is drugs."

He was so predictable. I had him in my crosshairs. "Well, Dad," I explained, "you know people shouldn't judge me for such things as the length of my hair. If they are going to be that judgmental, then I don't see why I should worry about it."

Surely now this ordeal would end. I was so compelling, so calm, so agreeable. I may even have harbored a small hope that I had done so well, that maybe he would grow his hair out a touch more, to show some solidarity with his wise and sensitive son. Instead, he called checkmate.

"Didn't you start out by saying that you grew your hair because of what you wanted people to think about you? And now you say you shouldn't care about what people will think about you!"

I had had many arguments with my father before that day. And I have had more than a few since then. But never have I experienced such an ignominious defeat. I was trounced, dead in the water. "Any barbershop will do," was how I cried uncle. I was ashamed, not of the length of my hair, but that I had missed such a glaring contradiction in my own thinking. It was then that I became a zealot not only for the Reformed faith, but for logic. Humiliation can do that.

I learned existentially then what I had heard my father say many times before: Logic serves as a truth cop. Its purpose is to go about the world of sloppy thinking and haul thought crimes off to prison. Thought crime, however, is not thinking ill of Big Brother, but thinking like a fool, thinking in contradictory terms. I had been busted, caught red-handed with a contradiction. I also learned then that logic was not the domain of an esoteric few. It was not an archaic art practiced by honored initiates. Rather, it was, and is, a part of all our thinking, all the time.

I've had the privilege of teaching logic to various groups of people, from teens to adults. I always ask my students to fold a piece of paper in thirds to construct a sort of nameplate to put on their desk until I learn all their names. But on the side that faces them, I ask them to write "Logic is not scary." I know that they are intimidated by logic, but also that that is an illogical fear. I explain to them that they already know a great deal about logic, but don't know that they know it, and that they are not going to learn a new way to think, but are going to learn consciously how they think unconsciously, at least when they are thinking well. I go on to explain that they are going to learn how to recognize those times when they and others are not thinking well, and how to demonstrate it. When we study logic, we must learn a lot of unfamiliar terms, but it is not a foreign language. It is the language of thought, and so it is universal.

As we think about logic as one of our necessities for intelligent thought, it is important to understand that logic is universal. We often speak about it as if it were not universal. When I point out that another person's view is illogical, I will often hear this defense: "Well, maybe it's not logical according to your logic, but it is according to my logic." While each of us may have our own peculiar brand of illogic, we do not have different brands of logic.

Is logic, then, some sort of universal law, a transcendent standard by which all truth is governed? Yes and no. It is a universal law, and it does transcend many things. All of the created order is beholden to it, but God is not. It does not transcend God. Logic does not have jurisdiction over God. But we have to be careful here. Often, when I appeal to logic in order to squelch an opponent's point of view, he thinks he has an escape route. "Well, yes," my opponent might say, "my understanding of man's free will does contradict my understanding of God's sovereignty. But you must understand that God's thoughts are not our thoughts, and his ways are not our ways. Man's free will and God's sovereignty are like two parallel lines that intersect in infinity. We can't understand it, but God can." The trouble with this line of thinking, this particular brand of illogic, is that it cannot be so. God is not subservient to the laws of logic, but neither does he transcend them. Even God cannot comprehend two parallel lines (that by definition never intersect) that intersect. Or, to put it another way, even God cannot make a square circle.

Each time I teach logic, after establishing that logic is not scary, I begin with the same question: "Can God make a rock so big that he cannot move it?" I enjoy listening to students hash it out. The larger party always says he can make such a rock, recognizing that to deny that he can make the rock is to deny his omnipotence. The smaller party sees the subtlety in the question, recognizing that to say that he can make such a rock also denies his omnipotence, because then there could be something that he could not move. When I first tried this, a young lady in the class seemed uninterested in the debate. As the two warring sides raised their voices to a fever pitch, she softly stated, "God can do all his holy will." That succinct answer, taken from the Westminster Confession of Faith, neatly explains the relationship between God and logic. God is neither above logic, such that he can make a square circle, nor below it, such that logic stands above God and forbids him to do so. Rather, logic is a part of the very nature of God. (One Christian philosopher, Gordon H. Clark, even argued that John 1:1 could be translated as "In the beginning was Logic." The Greek words usually translated "the Word" can also mean "logic.") He cannot make a rock so big that he cannot move it, not because he isn't strong enough, but because that would be at odds with his holy will. And it is his holy will to be a God of order, not of confusion.

If God were above logic, then we could not believe a word that he says. Logic begins with another fundamental and self-evident truth that philosophers like to wrangle over. It begins with the law of noncontradiction, which states, "Something cannot be both A and non-A at the same time and in the same relationship." This sounds simple because it is simple. It means simply that something cannot be one thing and not that thing at the same time and in the same relationship. Those last two qualifiers are important. For example, "I am a husband" is true today, yet "I am not a husband" was true fifteen years ago. That does not violate the law of noncontradiction, because the opposite statements were true at different times. Similarly, in relation to my wife, "I am a husband" is true, yet in relation to my children, "I am not a husband" is true. But these statements refer to different relationships.

I cannot be a husband to my wife and not a husband to my wife at the same time and in the same relationship. And God cannot say, "Believe on the Lord Jesus Christ and you shall be saved" and mean it, and at the same time say, "Believe on the Lord Jesus Christ and you shall be damned" and mean it. The law of noncontradiction prevents opposite statements from both being true. Again, there are no logic police waiting to club the Lord with a nightstick while he secretly itches to make a square circle or a really big rock. He is consistent. His word is truth, and so excludes falsehood.

Because God is a God of order, we can trust what he says. And if we, like him, are to be able to affirm any truth, we must operate within the realm of reality, which is within the realm of logic. There are those who, as by now you might suspect, would seek to deny that the rules of logic are necessarily valid. There are those who think it is the height of sophistication to contemplate the sound of one hand clapping. And naturally we cannot prove the necessity of using logic in our foundation of truth, because we would have no logic with which to do so. However, we can see that to deny logic is to affirm it. For instance, if I say, "It is not true that reality must be consistent with the law of noncontradiction," I am also saying at the same time and in the same relationship, "It is true that reality must be consistent with the law of noncontradiction." Without the law of noncontradiction in play to keep a thesis from turning into its antithesis, the thesis turns into its antithesis. The louder my opponent objects to having his own proposition turned into its opposite, the more he is insisting on the necessity of the law of noncontradiction. That is what we mean when we say that to deny the law of noncontradiction is to affirm it.

Our friends in the presuppositional camp have much the same problem. Just as they do not want to start with self-consciousness, so they do not want the laws of logic, including the law of noncontradiction, to be their starting point for knowledge. They want to start with God (who is, of course, logic). They insist on starting with God. But they do not start with God and cannot start with God. When my presuppositional brother says, "I do not start with logic; I start with God," my reply is always, "I'm delighted to hear that you now agree with me, that you do not start with God, but that you do start with logic." My opponent sometimes sees his dilemma at this point and sometimes needs further explanation: "If you do not have the law of noncontradiction in play, that is, if it is not operating because at your bedrock is God apart from logic, then how can you know that it isn't so that at the same time and in the same relationship there is no God at your bedrock. 'I start with God' equals 'I do not start with God' without the law of noncontradiction."

Anyone who wishes to make a case against the truthfulness of the laws of logic or their priority in the order of knowing, will be making an argument when they seek to make their case. That is, they will be trying to show, by aligning various propositions in logical order, that their conclusion is in fact true and valid. Like the behaviorist who argues rationally with us to persuade us that our ideas do not come from rational argumentation, but rather from our environment, so the irrationalist will try to argue rationally that reason doesn't tell us what is true and what is false.

Or he may argue in a different way. He may begin to make his case against consistency and coherency in a more consistent and coherent way. He may say, "Of course I cannot prove to you in a logical manner why logic doesn't reflect reality. I can't give you reasons for rejecting reasons. That wouldn't make any sense, which would be right, because nothing makes any sense. The world, and therefore my own position regarding the world, is irrational and incoherent." To deny the validity of reason is to sink into nihilism. There can be no truth, if there can be no way to distinguish it from falsehood. And when one describes one's view as being irrational and incoherent, it is therefore indefensible, and so the argument is over.

In noting the necessity of starting with the rules of logic, we are not making a gratuitous leap. There is a sense in which we are not presupposing anything as such. The rules of logic are, at base, without content. They are the very form of arguments, without being arguments themselves. They are empty containers that give shape to whatever we put in them. There are other rules of logic that are as necessary as the law of noncontradiction—necessary in the sense that they must be so, and necessary in the sense that we cannot understand our world without them. There are, for instance, what are called the laws of immediate inference. For example, we know that if all A are B, then some A are B. And if no A are B, then some A are not B. We know that if all A are B, then it cannot be so that no A are B. It doesn't matter what you fill in for A or B in any of these formulas. It is as valid to say that if all apples are bruised, then some apples are bruised, as it is to say that if all argons are blaffie, then some argons are blaffie. That is why we say that logic is devoid of content.

We cannot negotiate with the rules of logic. We cannot proceed without them. If they are not part of our starting point, we cannot start. We don't have to be able to name them, or even be aware that we are using them. I explain to my students at the beginning of my logic classes that they will not find themselves in situations where they think, "Now I will use the logic that I have learned," as you might apply some algebra that you have learned. Rather, logic simply sets forth how our brains work when they are working well. Just as Descartes did not invent self-consciousness, so Aristotle did not invent logic. When Adam heard God say, "Of this tree you may not eat," he had to know that this did not also mean, at the same time and in the same relationship, "Of this tree you may eat."

We do make errors in our use of logic. We draw conclusions that do not follow from the premises that we have been given. Sin has profoundly affected our minds. But it has not affected logic. Logic is not a by-product of our fallen minds, but a tool used rightly (logically) or wrongly (illogically) by our fallen minds. We could not know that we had made an error in our thinking, in our logic, if we did not have logic to serve as our judge. The same thing happens even with math. Suppose I add 1 and 2 and 3 and 4 and 5 and come up with 16. I have made an error in my addition. But I would not know I have made that error unless it were possible for my mind to add the numbers together rightly and see that they add up to 15. If I say, "All men are mortal; Socrates is mortal; therefore Socrates is a man," that may sound logical enough. But I see that I have committed a fallacy (the fallacy of the undistributed middle) if I keep the same form of argument, but substitute other terms: "All cats have four legs; my dog Socks has four legs; therefore my dog Socks is a cat." Logical error, in other words, does not prove that logic cannot be trusted. Instead, it shows that we must depend upon logic against illogic.

I cannot prove the validity of logic, because I would not be able to use the unproved logic as the tool to do so. It too comes under our epistemic dilemma. But I hope I have shown that without it we can know nothing, that it is a necessary precondition for knowing anything. I hope also that I have shown that to deny the validity of logic is at the same time to affirm it. This is how we know things. We start with ourselves, self-consciousness, and move on to the logic that makes knowledge possible. This is how God has made us. Logic is not the god above God, but a gift from God so that we might have real knowledge about real things, including the very God who gave us the gift in the first place.

## CHAPTER TWELVE

# TO SEE OR NOT TO SEE

R eason or logic, you will remember, is, at base, devoid of content. It is like a gelatin mold, which itself contains no gelatin, but gives shape to the gelatin that is placed in it. If reason is a good mold, and it is, then it will give the proper shape to whatever is put into it. Reason will order our thoughts when we are thinking as God thinks, in a rational and coherent way. But we still have to get the thoughts into the form, the gelatin into the mold. In chapter 3, we took great pains to make what is in one sense a rather subtle distinction, between brain and mind. We argued that there must be something about our thinking that is both real and not chemical, something that is not reducible to either matter or energy. What we didn't do, and what is not only outside the scope of this book, but beyond the scope of my ability, is to explain exactly how the world outside us intersects with our own minds. What we will see is that they do intersect, even if we do not know how.

This question, like so many others in philosophy, is one that we don't often consider in our everyday lives. That there is a world outside us, and that we can know real things about it, is what we call common sense. But, as we have seen, one of the first things people jettison from their worldview when trying to escape the claims of God on their life is common sense. Several of the best and brightest in the history of philosophy have expended great energy trying to make the case that we cannot have any real knowledge of the world around us.

We have talked about how modern philosophy was originally, in large part, a debate between rationalists and empiricists. The former said that all knowledge comes through the right application of reason. The latter insisted instead that knowledge comes to us through our senses. When neither side prevailed, modern skepticism arose. But that deadlock might also be understood as a double loss. Neither side could win because the other side kept poking holes in their arguments. Each did a fine job of destroying the other, but neither could make their own case. The empiricists kept insisting that you can get nothing into the mold without your senses, while the rationalists kept insisting that your gelatin will spill all over the floor without the mold. Without a rational mind to make sense of all the data that we receive through our senses, we have, of course, an undifferentiated mass of data, a blob. There is nothing that comes through my senses that makes me know the difference between the white on this page and the black on this page. It takes a mind to see that the letters are distinct from the paper, and that the letters come together to form words

that communicate ideas. My senses alone fail me because I cannot make sense of what they see without a
mind to order it. In like manner, no matter how rational
my arguments may be, they cannot pass from me to you
except through our senses, in this case, your eyes reading
these words.

The solution is to understand that both the mind and
the senses are necessary for understanding. We do not fault
half a circle for not being a whole circle. Neither should we
fault one part of how we know things for not being complete in itself. The empiricists are right that without our
senses there is little if anything to know. It's all well and
good to know that A cannot be both A and *non-A* at the
same time and in the same relationship, but it doesn't really
mean anything until we plug something into the A. And
the rationalists are right that without reason we cannot
know anything about what we experience. But with both
principles operating as first principles, we can know that we
can see, and can see that we can know.

My goal in this chapter is to give some credence to the
empiricist side of the argument. I deny with the rationalists
that we can know things with our senses alone. I affirm,
however, that our senses are basically reliable, and that,
with our rational minds at work ordering our sense experience, our senses can give us genuine information about the
world around us. We can know something, though not
everything, about reality. I cannot present a compelling rational argument for the basic reliability of our senses. I cannot do so for the same reasons that I could not do so for the
laws of logic. I would be assuming the basic reliability of our

senses in order to make the case for the basic reliability of our senses. The basic reliability of our senses is so foundational that there is no foundation below it to support it. It is one of our first principles of knowing. But, as with the laws of logic, I can demonstrate that to deny the basic reliability of our senses is necessarily to assume the basic reliability of our senses. And the argument is made in essentially the same way as it is with logic.

I have conversations with people who would deny the basic reliability of their senses. Not one of them has ever been earnest. Instead, each of them wants an excuse to deny what they already know. Their senses tell them, through the witness of God in the created order, that there is a God, that they are answerable to him, and that they have failed to measure up to his standard of righteousness. They are looking for a way out. Nevertheless, they argue, "How can you say that our senses are basically reliable? Our senses are not basically reliable." I always give the same response: "I'm delighted to hear that you agree with me that our senses are basically reliable. Indeed, you are right, the conclusion is inescapable." In most cases, my poor friend has no idea what happened. He usually simply trudges on: "No, you didn't hear what I said. I said I *don't* agree that our senses are basically reliable." "Yes, yes," I reply, "I'm glad to see you so zealous for the cause of truth, and all that. And believe me, I'm encouraged by your insistent and loud affirmation of what I have just said, but really it is time to move on." At this point, my friend realizes that I did hear his objection, and that my response was intended to be a parry. If I really feel like having fun, I might point over my friend's shoulder and shriek, "Run for your life, it's a man-eating lion!" Never has a skeptic doubted his own senses enough to flee from a lion that his eyes cannot see.

If necessary, I then proceed to explain my response. To make the claim that our senses are not basically reliable is to assume that our senses are basically reliable. When we make an argument, we do it either by writing it down in a book or an essay, which is then brought before the minds of others through the senses, or we speak it out loud. When we speak the argument, we assume it is audible. When we write the argument down, we assume that it is visible—or will be, once it is printed. It does not matter what the argument is. It could be unfathomably complex or astoundingly simple. It could be whispered or shouted, written in blue ink or black, or written across the Montana sky by a skywriter. It could be reduced to braille or American Sign Language. But for it to pass from one mind to another, it must pass through our senses. There is no idea, including the idea that our senses are unreliable, or any argument in support of that idea, that can be communicated without the use of our senses.

The empirical skeptic cannot live consistently with his own affirmations. He has to deny that the hands that he sees actually feel. He has to deny that the eyes that he touches actually see. Even if he is wise enough to know that to make his case is to deny it, he still must make choices. Even if he is not having an argument with me, he is doing something. (He cannot even know that he is not trying to make the argument. The fact that he does not hear his voice making an argument is meaningless, if he cannot trust his senses. If he does not feel his lips move, he still cannot know that he is not talking.) He can either stay in the room that may or may not have a man-eating lion in it, or he can go into another room, which may also contain a man-eating lion. He can walk between the rooms either by stepping through the doorway that his eyes perceive or by stepping through the wall that his untrustworthy eyes say is right in front of him. If he wants, he can try to deny that his nose hurts, but he must decide whether to put ice on it or not. If he determines that his nose is in need of care, and so heads off to the emergency room, he must decide whether to believe that the stop sign says "Stop" or not to believe it. If he doesn't believe it, he must decide whether or not there really is a policeman behind him with sirens blaring. However, he has no basis on which to make his decisions. There is no more reason to believe that the policeman is there than there is to believe that he is not there. There is no more reason to stop than there is to go.

In short, if there were a consistent empirical skeptic, he would no doubt be a close friend of our consistent nihilist, Bartleby. He could not base any decisions on any ideas that come to him through his senses. He would live, if he could, the life of the mind alone. And he would live it alone. He would be the ultimate solipsist, and you would never need to worry about debating with him. He might spend his life in a sensory deprivation tank, but if our senses are unreliable, they are unreliable whether they are turned off or on. How would he know that he was in the tank, when his senses could be telling him he was in the tank when he was actually in the jaws of a man-eating lion? Perhaps a better friend for our empirical skeptic might be Nietzsche after he had lost his mind.

The better approach for the skeptic to take in attacking the basic reliability of our senses is to attack that hedge word that sticks out like a sore thumb. I have not been arguing that our senses are perfectly reliable, but rather that they are basically reliable. We have all been fooled by our senses. Few of us have seen a mirage of an oasis while crawling across the desert sand, but most of us have seen things that we later discovered were not as they seemed. When I go to the funhouse at the carnival, and I stand in front of one of those odd mirrors, I do not shriek in delight that I have miraculously grown six inches taller and lost six inches around my waist. When I look up at a jet passing overhead, and I hear it later than I see it, I do not fear that the fabric of the universe is unraveling. When I dip my oar into the water, I do not fear that it has broken because of the bend I see in it. Things are not always as they appear to be.

Because we have experienced such discrepancies between what our senses seem to tell us and what actually happens, it is important to use that hedge word. But it is also important to recognize that the hedge does not undo the thing we are hedging. These experiences do not disprove the proposition that our senses are basically reliable. They are, instead, merely the empirical equivalent of errors in logic. In the last chapter, we were careful to affirm that there is no such thing as "man's logic." There are only logic and illogic. We conceded that we sometimes make mistakes in our logic. We jump to conclusions or commit assorted fallacies. Those mistakes, however, do not disprove the validity of logic; rather, they support logic. We can recognize that we have made a logical error only by applying logic rightly to the issue at hand.

Our senses work in the same way. Suppose I see myself in a funhouse mirror. I would suspect that my eyes were deceiving me, because I know from experience that people do not change their shape in such a radical way simply by standing in front of a peculiar mirror. To confirm that my eyes were tricking me, I could do any number of things. I could use a tape measure to see if my waist had actually shrunk. I could use a yardstick to measure my height. When I see that the numbers are the same (which I will not divulge here), I will know that my eyes have deceived me. But I will know it through the use of my eyes. Similarly, if I run my hand along the length of my oar while it looks bent in the water, I will feel that it is not bent. I will test one of my senses with another of my senses. When I watch the jet in the sky, I will use my mind to compare the time that the sound takes to get to me with the time that it should take for a sound to get to me from the jet, and discover that the sound is actually coming from the jet.

Our earlier rejoinder will also work. If these examples of times when our senses seem to fool us are given to me by the skeptic, they are once more given to me through our senses. The skeptic must rely on the basic reliability of our senses to make his case against their basic reliability.

The basic reliability of our senses is of necessity a foundational truth. Yet sometimes it is not skeptics, but believers, who try to deny this reality. If I affirm that the most foundational part of all my knowing is the Bible, I have the same problem as the empirical skeptic. In one sense, the Bible is the most foundational source of truth. But to get to the truth in the Bible, we again need our senses. If our senses are not basically reliable, we cannot know what the Bible says. If the basic reliability of our senses is not established first, we cannot trust that the Bible actually teaches their basic reliability. The Bible, instead, assumes that our senses are reliable and then proceeds to tell us about the God of grace and order who gave us our senses in the first place.

We have our senses only because the God of the Bible gave them to us. His being precedes ours and is the source of our knowing things through the senses he gave us. We know that without him, we could not trust our senses. But without our trustworthy senses, we could not know about him, through reading his revelation to us, whether it be through his word or through his creation.

This does not mean, of course, that we take an empirical approach to the question of God's existence. I am not suggesting that I will believe in God only when he shows himself. One thing our senses tell us in the Bible is that the second he shows himself, we all die, for no man can see God and live. The God of the Bible, we know, is spirit. But we know that he is spirit because our eyes have shown us the very words of God in the Bible.

We cannot know if our senses fail us, because to know the truth that contrasts with what our senses are telling us, we would need to trust our senses. Our dependence on the basic reliability of our senses, then, is unprovable, but inescapable. But because God has given us our senses, and because he has made them reliable, we can know about his world and about him.

## CHAPTER THIRTEEN

# GJTTY

In order for us to have knowledge, and in order for us to be able to communicate the knowledge we have, we must live in a universe in which the laws of logic rule. Any universe in which A can be both A and *non-A* at the same time and in the same relationship is a universe in which we can affirm nothing and deny nothing, including the assertion that A can be both A and *non-A* at the same time and in the same relationship. We must also live in a universe in which we can basically trust what our senses tell us. Even to speak of lying senses is to speak with a trust in our senses. Relativists and other skeptics, of course, seek to deny both of these nonnegotiables for truth. The relativist tells us that if we believe that Jesus is the Son of God, then for us he is the Son of God. To him, however, Jesus is not the Son of God. Note that we are not talking about a change in relationship. I am affirming what Jesus is, apart from my affirmation. He is denying what I affirm, and yet claims that both my affirmation and his denial are true. He is saying that A can be both A and *non-A* at the same time and in the same relationship, which is also to say that A cannot be both A and *non-A* at the same time and in the same relationship.

If I make the claim that I am seven feet tall, the relativist is not content to get out the yardstick and prove me wrong. There is no wrong, and there is no proof in the relativist world. Instead, he will say that if I so believe, it is so. He will deny that the message I receive from my senses, which says that I am well short of seven feet tall, is accurate. And, like Alice in Wonderland, if I next believe I am seven inches tall, it will be so, to me. I cannot rely on my senses. Reality is what I construct in my own mind. If I believe something, it is so, for me.

The relativist denies that any truth is objectively true, and affirms that every "truth" is either true for me or not. But it is not only propositions that are destroyed by relativism, but also the very tools by which propositions are made. Not only can any statement mean whatever we want it to mean, but each of the words in a statement can mean whatever we want it to mean. One does not have to be a sophisticated philosopher to make this claim. In fact, one of the earliest proponents of this view was a rather rotten egg. Lewis Carroll, in his children's tale *Alice Through the Looking Glass*, recounts a conversation between young Alice and Humpty Dumpty:

> "I don't know what you mean by 'glory,' "
> Alice said.
> Humpty Dumpty smiled contemptuously. "Of

course you don't—till I tell you. I meant 'there's a
nice knock-down argument for you!' "

"But *glory* doesn't mean 'a nice knock-down argument,' " Alice objected.

"When I use a word," Humpty Dumpty said, in
a rather scornful tone, "it means just what I choose
it to mean—neither more nor less."

"The question is," said Alice, "whether you
can make words mean so many different things."

"The question is," said Humpty Dumpty,
"which is to be the master—that's all."

Alice is here fighting for the angels, while Humpty
Dumpty is obviously cracked. Words, in order to communicate, must mean what they are commonly understood
to mean. But there are those who wish them to mean
something altogether different. In fact, there has perhaps
never been a time when words were abused as much as
they are now.

Ironically, if Humpty Dumpty is right, he and Alice
may actually be in agreement. Humpty Dumpty promises
that Alice will know what he meant by "glory" when he has
a chance to explain it to her. But in order to explain what
he meant by "glory," he has to use words, to which he
claims the right to assign meaning. To put it another way,
what does Humpty Dumpty mean by "a nice knock-down
argument"? It may have nothing to do with people disagreeing and everything to do with whatever it is that Alice understands glory to be. If words mean whatever we
want them to mean, we cannot explain our meaning and

communicate with others, for we can only explain our meaning with words, which in turn need to be explained by words, *ad infinitum.*

Every political season, at least for the last decade or so, we have witnessed candidates on both sides of the political fence doing all they can to demonstrate to the voting public that they are all for "family values." That expression is a curious one. It doesn't really tell us anything. What exactly are family values? Is the command to love our neighbor a family value, or is it the law of God? If it is a family value, does that mean that single people are exempt from it? If it is not a family value, does that mean that we should be against it? The phenomenon exists because *family* is considered a good word. Quite apart from what it actually means, it carries positive connotations with it. And so every candidate seeks to get that word associated with his or her campaign. Professing conservatives have an easier time holding onto the label. The left, despite its support of the homosexual agenda, still at least tries to hold onto the term. One bumper sticker states, "Hate is not a family value." Here is an attempt to recapture *family* from the conservatives and to pin the bad word *hate* on them.

This is not all empty rhetoric, however. Words not only have meanings, but power. Keeping words and their meanings together has an important purpose. If *family* can mean whatever you want it to mean, then why shouldn't homosexuals (who have completely captured the word *gay*) be able to have benefits for their "domestic partners"? If marriage can mean whatever you want it to mean, how can we try to stop homosexuals from getting married? Whether

the human embryo is an unborn child or an undifferentiated blob of tissue can make a profound difference in how
we look at the abortion debate. If we recognize that homosexual unions are an abomination, and that abortion is
murder, we are still abusing the language if we express our
"outrage" as merely being "for family values." If "conservatives" refuse to call a spade a spade, they should not be surprised that liberals will not, either.

However, words lose their power when they lose their
meaning. I am using nothing but words in my attempt to
help people tear down strongholds. And the strongholds we
are to tear down, the arguments we are to cast aside, are
also made up of nothing but words. But that is not nothing.
Words have power, not in the sense that if we say them this
way or that, we can work magic, but in the sense that they
actually communicate. The very fall of mankind can be
traced to an attack on the ability of words to communicate.
When the devil asked, "Has God said . . . ?" he challenged
the words of God.

The attack on the ability of words to communicate is
part and parcel of the attack on truth as made by relativists.
Humpty Dumpty gives us a clue as to what motivates those
who are making the attack. His question is which is to be
master. Will we bow to the meanings of words, or will we
seize the authority to grant those meanings? Will we submit
to God's reality, the only real reality, or will we be kings in
castles in the clouds? That is the issue.

Our purpose here, however, is not to argue that it is
important that we agree that words have meanings, and
that those meanings are important. Rather, we want to af-

firm that words are able to communicate, and that their ability to communicate is a necessary precondition for knowing any truth. Once again, we cannot prove that words are able to communicate. Such proof would require two things that are not at our disposal: a more fundamental building block of knowing, and words that we know can communicate. That is, we are laying down the prerequisites for knowledge. And we cannot use words to prove that words can communicate if we do not yet know that words can communicate.

However, we can demonstrate that to deny the premise that words can communicate is at the same time to affirm the premise that words can communicate. Our method is again essentially the same as before. Suppose someone objects to this premise and declares, "Words are not able to communicate." What is the goal of the person raising this counterclaim? What does he hope to accomplish? He desires to let it be known that he believes that words cannot communicate. And he has communicated this desire with words. In raising the counterclaim, he has affirmed the premise in question. In fact, it would seem that his best hope of communicating his disagreement with the premise would be to communicate agreement with it.

Once again, the person who sincerely holds to the idea that words cannot communicate should have no reason to speak or write. Even if this person believed in the validity of the laws of logic and in the basic reliability of our senses, he would have to be mute. One need never fear facing a sincere Humpty Dumpty in debate. A sincere Humpty Dumpty is a silent Humpty Dumpty, even before he has a great fall. And after his fall, he cannot even thank all the king's men for trying to put him together again.

While it does not take a philosopher to get into this kind of trouble, it certainly helps. The notion that words cannot communicate has taken hold most firmly among academics, most powerfully among professors of language. Relativism when "practiced" in the field of literature is known as deconstructionism, which is the dominant view at Western universities. Deconstructionism begins by deconstructing aesthetics, arguing that there is no objective measure of beauty. I witnessed the fruit of this notion while studying English in graduate school, where one of my professors explained, "A laundry list is as much literature as Shakespeare." There was, in his view, no objective standard by which we could judge the artistic merits of Shakespeare over against the laundry list.

Deconstructionism next deconstructs ethics by arguing for cultural relativism. Here too the canon of Western literature is attacked, simply because it is Western. Thus, Shakespeare is no more literature than the ancient cave drawings of primitive peoples. We cannot say that Homer's honoring of honor is any better or worse than the celebration of adultery in *The Tale of Genji*. Finally, the assault reaches truth itself and the ability of words to communicate truth. Deconstructionists argue that there is no meaning inherent in the text. In other words, Humpty Dumpty can not only make his own words mean whatever he wants them to mean, but also make Alice's words mean whatever he wants them to mean. The reader, and not the writer, is the one who brings meaning to the text.

Here again, however, they don't really believe this. While I was in graduate school, I had the privilege of teaching freshman English. I took a class that was designed to help me learn how to teach this introduction to literature and writing. As my professor explained that there was no inherent meaning in the text, that one interpretation was as good as any other, I asked the obvious question, "How then are we supposed to grade? If one student says that Hamlet's soliloquy was all about the struggles in this life against injustice, and the question of whether we enter a better world after our death, and another suggests that this famous speech is actually about the difficulty horses have in determining whether they prefer red apples to green apples, how am I to judge them? If there is no right answer, there can be no wrong answer." My professor explained that while there was no right answer, some were better than others. Or, to put it another way, while there was no target, some were closer to it than others. Sadly, I never had the courage to posit the apple theory in any of the classes I took, so I could challenge the foolishness of deconstructionism more seriously.

Douglas Wilson, in his magazine *Credenda/Agenda*, published a story years ago about a pair of courageous students. The setting was a guest lecture given by a character who represented Stanley Fish, a professor at Duke University who was one of the leaders of deconstructionism. After he completed his lecture, in which he explained that we could make words mean whatever we wanted them to mean, he opened the floor for questions. A young lady said, "That was a fine lecture, Professor, but I'm curious how you think it is safe to come in here and argue that white civilization was superior to that of the native Americans." Fish objected that he said no such thing. "And then to say that women are the weaker sex was just going too far, Professor." The professor looked about the auditorium for help. "Did anybody hear me say anything of this sort?" The young lady's partner raised his hand. "No, sir, of course not. You said no such thing. You did, however, sexually harass my girlfriend, and I'm going to have to report you." The professor was trying to have his cake and eat it too, claiming the authority to give words meaning, but objecting when his words were the object of such abuse.

The abuse of language, though it is well ensconced in the ivory tower, is not isolated to that environment. We witness it daily in the field of marketing. The other day I ordered a pizza by phone from a national chain. I asked for a medium-sized pizza. The poor soul taking my order had to explain that they had no medium pizzas there. They only had small, large, and extra-large. If you've ever had to buy laundry detergent, you've been through the same thing. Only there there is no small size—only large, jumbo, and (here we go again) family value size.

It seems to be great fun to have power over words, to be able to make them mean whatever you want them to mean. It can also be rather effective, at least for a while. Some marketers, like politicians, seek to harness the power of words, all the while draining them of their power by using them wrongly. This gives rise to what might be called language inflation. Our words no longer carry the meaning that they once carried, so we need bigger and grander

words. Our superlatives become anemic from overuse. Soon
we need to hype our product as stupendous, because to call
it merely great is to damn it with faint praise. Soon we find
that those who give merely 100 percent effort are pikers,
those who give 110 percent are average, and those who give
150 percent are really hustling. In the end, however, we
end up with the Tower of Babel. When words no longer
mean anything, they can no longer convey meaning from
one mind to another. Once again, the relativism that was
supposed to allow us to live in peace together has instead
divided us, as we are all exiled to our own solipsistic world
of unbridgeable loneliness.

Our believing friends who insist that we must start
with the Bible have the same problem here as they had
with our other two nonnegotiables. First, one cannot
even speak the words "I start with the Bible," if we have
not first established that words can communicate. I respond to that claim, "I'm glad you agree that we have to
start with the ability of words to communicate, before we
come to the words of the Bible." To object to my assign-
ing of my own meaning to the words of my opponent is
to affirm that words have meaning apart from either the
speaker or the hearer. Second, the Bible cannot be understood if words cannot communicate. If we do not affirm that words communicate before we read the first
word of the Bible, then we can never know what the
Bible is telling us. It is because words have the ability to
communicate that the Word is able to communicate with
us. It is because the God of the universe made it the way
that he did that we can hear from him. Words are not

sovereign over God, but God uses real words to convey real meaning.

The truth is that words do communicate. They communicate either truthfully or falsely. There is no other option. Truth is still "what is," and when we speak what is, we speak the truth. When we speak what is not, we speak falsely, no matter how much we might want to believe it. Words have power, but when they are used outside of their real meaning, they have only the power to deceive. That some use them that way, however, does not change the fact that they can communicate. Again, if someone objects that since all men are liars and so many abuse words, we therefore cannot use words to communicate, their objection should fall on us as if our ears were deaf. We hear the objection and understand it, precisely because it is invalid. Just as we do not need to show the irrationality of those who deny reason, or need to converse with those who deny the power of their senses, so we do not need to silence those fools who have silenced themselves.

## CHAPTER FOURTEEN

# THE GOD WHO IS THERE

'm not the handiest man in the world. My father taught me many things, for which I am grateful, but how to use a hammer was not one of them. My wife's father, on the other hand, is handy. And so my wife expects me to be able to fix things and build things just as her father does. The result is that every Christmas and every birthday, every Father's Day, and some Valentine's Days, I receive tools from my wife. I have two toolboxes full of tools. The trouble is that the tools, as useful as they might be, are rather useless in my untrained hands. I'm okay with a sledgehammer, but just because it is used for breaking things to pieces rather than piecing things together. Tools are nice, but they are not an end in themselves. They exist for something outside themselves.

In the first part of this book, we took a sledgehammer to false ideas about how we know things. In the last several chapters, we have considered the tools that God has given us so that we might know things. In the first part, we saw how some oftentimes brilliant people have used the minds God has given them to try to escape from the claims of God on their lives. Now we will consider how God's gifts of knowing lead us to know the Giver.

Thomas Aquinas is perhaps best known for his arguments for the existence of God. He set forth several arguments, including the teleological argument (arguing from design in the world to God's existence—the clockmaker argument), an ontological argument (arguing from being to God's existence) that was somewhat different from Anselm's ontological argument, and a moral argument (arguing from a universal moral code to God's existence). Aquinas's major contribution to apologetics, however, was not in coming up with new arguments. Instead, the man who was known in his youth as the dumb ox helped the church by systematizing arguments that had been around for some time. The cosmological argument, one could argue, had been around since the creation of man. It is in essence the same argument that Paul makes in Romans:

> For the wrath of God is revealed from heaven against all ungodliness and unrighteousness of men, who suppress the truth in unrighteousness, because what may be known of God is manifest in them, for God has shown it to them. For since the creation of the world His invisible attributes are clearly seen, being understood by the things that are made, even His eternal power and Godhead, so that they are without excuse. (1:18–20)

Paul is saying that all men know (although they continually suppress that knowledge) that the Creator exists, despite his being invisible, because they can see his magnificent creation, the world around them. Paul is not constructing a new argument for God's existence, but rather is repeating an argument that had existed since man first marveled at the world around him. That men seek to suppress this knowledge is no evidence that the argument is invalid. That men are left without excuse is powerful evidence that it is valid.

However, if God has made himself known to all men through the creation, why do some not believe? If the argument is compelling, why are not all compelled to believe? If God exists, why are there atheists? We need to understand the vital distinction between proof and persuasion. Proof is objective; persuasion is subjective. When we prove something to be true, we demonstrate that it must be so. When we persuade, we get someone to agree with what we are saying. If I argue, for instance, that all dogs are animals, and that my dog Socks is a dog, and therefore that Socks is an animal, I have proved my case. Someone, however, might have a vested interest in denying that Socks is an animal. Perhaps one of my children is so bent on allowing Socks to live in the house, that he refuses to accept that she is an animal. I have proved my case, but have failed to persuade my child—who has likewise failed to persuade me to let the dog in the house.

Sinners have a perceived vested interest in denying the existence of the one true God. If he exists, they are beholden to him. If he exists and is holy, but they are not holy, then they must face his wrath. While Freud, Marx, and others have suggested that we believe in God because it makes us feel better to do so, the truth is that there is nothing more frightening than the living God. He is not something we would make up for our pleasure, although he is something we might seek to deny. Because we have ulterior motives, we are not always persuaded of what has been proved. The arguments that follow, I pray, will not only prove God's existence, but may, through the regenerating work of the Holy Spirit, bring peace between him and those who are at war with him.

We begin with the truth that something exists. We know first that we exist, because to deny or even to doubt our own existence, we first must be. We know also that there is a world around us. We may not know much about ourselves or about the world, but we know that these things exist. Their existence means that we or the universe must be (1) eternal or self-created, (2) created by something eternal, or (3) created by something created. If we choose the third alternative, we merely move the question back a step. If the universe was created by something created, then how was the thing that created us created? In the end, we must either accept our second alternative, that the first created thing was created by an eternal thing, or we must affirm an infinite chain of finite causes, stretching back into eternity.

The trouble with this last option is that it is still too early. It is called an "infinite regress." While we might conceive of an infinite chain of contingent causes, we cannot conceive of the time in which those causes would be operating. We know that it takes a week to get through a week. A week ago, when we looked forward to this day, we knew that, barring the end of the world, in seven days this day would be here. But how long would it take to cross through eternity? If there is no beginning, then time has been running forever, eternally. But you cannot cross eternity. That is what I mean by suggesting that it is too early. You can no more make it through an infinite number of yesterdays than you can count from negative infinity to zero, even if you had an infinite amount of time in which to do it. Even God himself cannot traverse an infinite past. We affirm that God precedes time, that there was never a time when he was not, though he existed when time was not.

This theory of an infinite regress, while utter nonsense, has historically been rather common. Primitive cultures would postulate that the world was resting on the back of a turtle, which was standing on an elephant, which was standing on something else, *ad infinitum.* Some scientists say that we are in the midst of an eternally expanding and contracting universe. The universe dissipates until it begins to contract. It squeezes itself back into a point of singularity, and then explodes outward, until it begins to dissipate again. This, however, tells us nothing about our origin. It only tells us, if it's true, about what's been going on for a while, because, again, if it has been going on forever, it cannot get to today.

Perhaps the most common form of nonsense that seeks to explain the cause of the effect that is the universe around us, is that it created itself. Sometimes the so-called big bang theory is expressed in this way, that the universe, at some point in the distant past, exploded into being. Self-creation, however, is nothing but irrational foolishness. It is a contradiction in terms. In order for the universe to do the work of creating itself, it would, of course, first have to be. It would have to be before it was. There is no universe in existence to create the universe. Even God, who is all-powerful, could not pull that one off. He couldn't create himself, for he would not be there to do the job. (And he could not create himself for another reason: God, by definition, is uncreated.)

Both of our remaining options require something that is eternal, something that has the power of being within itself. We have, in some sense, already established that there is some sort of supreme being, a being that is not dependent, derived, or contingent, that is a power unto itself. What we have not yet determined is whether this being is the universe (the option which says that the universe is eternal) or transcends the universe. And if it is the latter, we have not determined whether this eternal entity is a personal or impersonal being.

However, we can narrow our options down still further. We can know, for instance, that the universe is not eternal. We know this because it changes, and that which changes, by virtue of its changing, is not eternal. Suppose I were to posit that the computer on which I am writing is eternal, that it has always existed. We know this to be false because only one hundred years ago there was no such thing as a computer. Not many years ago, the material making up the computer in front of me was probably a pile of silicon on some beach somewhere, from which the chips were made, a puddle of crude oil somewhere else, from which the plastic was formed, and a pinch of assorted ores from various places, from which the electronic components were made. A hundred years ago, the languages my computer "speaks" did not even exist in the minds of men.

The same is true for each of us. We cannot be the eternal creator of all things because we change. I used to be thin. I was even tall for my age for a while. Now I am neither of those things. I used to fear computers, now I merely have a healthy respect for them. The "I" that I am now is not the same "I" that I was even yesterday. Now I am a day older and a day more decayed. By the time this reaches you, if I am still alive, I will be older and balder still. If the question is raised, "Did R. C. Jr. create the universe?" the next question needs to be "Which one?" It cannot be the R. C. Jr. of today, because I was a different R. C. Jr. yesterday.

There is, however, a part of me that does not change. That's part of what we mean by identity. I remember the thin me as me, and I'm still, in some sense, the same guy. My computer may not always have been a computer, but the silicon has been silicon for a while, and the crude oil, which used to be a dinosaur or some such thing, was made up of atoms that have not changed. If we look beyond the things that change, and find instead some steady, unchanging part of the universe, that has the power of being within itself, then we have found God. God is that or he which is self-existent, independent, and unchangeable. God is transcendent.

Transcendence, however, is not an attribute of geography. When we postulate this unchanging, eternal core of the universe as the source of all things, the unbeliever objects that this is just a part of the universe, that it does not stand outside the universe. But he is confused about transcendence. When we say that God is transcendent, or above the universe, we are not saying that if one were to climb to the top the universe, and then take a few steps beyond it, he would be with God. God's transcendence is ontological, pertaining to his being, not to his location. God is transcendent because he is a higher order of being, and he is a higher order of being precisely because he is not contingent, derived, or dependent, but alone has the power of being within himself. Because either we ourselves or the universe exists, something must have the power of being within itself. That is the essence of our cosmological argument. It is also the essence of the argument that Paul describes in Romans 1. We have not yet established that this supreme being is the God of the Bible, but we have established that there is a supreme being who, like the God of the Bible, must be eternal, unchangeable, and the source of all created things.

Our argument is built around a simple extension of the most fundamental rule of logic, the law of noncontradiction. That extension is the law of causality, which says that every effect must have a sufficient cause. That's a careful way of saying both that you can't get something for nothing and that you get what you pay for. The universe, or we ourselves, the effects, must have a cause. And ultimately there must be one cause that is not also an effect, which has the power of being in itself or himself.

That same rule of logic can help us see still more about

this self-existent, immutable being. It can tell us that this being is not impersonal, but personal. We all have an understanding of the hierarchy of being. We know, for instance, that a self-existent being is transcendent over a being that was made by, and is dependent upon, that self-existent being. Beings that live are a higher order of being than those that do not. A plant is a higher order of being than a rock, for instance. Beings with volition are a higher order of being than beings without volition, and so a rabbit is a higher order of being than a plant. And beings with self-consciousness or personhood are a higher order of being than those without, so that a human being is a higher order of being than a rabbit.

Perhaps you see where we're headed. With the laws of logic, it is important to be precise. The law of causality is not merely that every effect has a cause, but that every effect has a *sufficient* cause. The cause or causes must have sufficient power to produce the effect. You cannot get more from less. It follows that since we have self-consciousness, that which created us must also have self-consciousness. The creator cannot be an impersonal force, but must be personal. The fact that we can communicate means that he must be able to communicate.

We have not demonstrated, and indeed cannot demonstrate, that the God who is described in the Bible is this supreme being. However, we have eliminated the possibility that there could be no god. Of course, in the United States most people still believe in some sort of god. But we have also eliminated any notion of a god that is an impersonal force. And everything that we have deduced about

God is utterly consistent with what we learn about God in the Bible.

Some of my friends who want to begin by presupposing the existence of the God of the Bible, find this disappointing. It is not, however, disappointing for Paul. Recall that when he makes the same basic argument in Romans 1, he lists two things that all men know from the existence of the universe about the Creator of the universe. They know his eternal godhead and power. They know that God is self-existent eternally, and that God is sovereign over all things. Paul's argument, however, is not that all men know that there is a being who has attributes that characterize the true God, but which might also characterize some other being. Rather, in knowing these two attributes, men know the God who is, so that they are without excuse. The existence of the universe, whether it is used as the building block of the argument in this chapter or not, is enough to prove compellingly that the God of the universe exists, and that he is the one true God. It is even enough, in a sense, to be a compelling argument. Paul says that all men reach the same conclusion, but that all men, without the regenerating work of the Holy Spirit, suppress that knowledge.

There is another way to get at the same conclusion— a different, but similar argument put forth by those who suggest that they begin their knowing by presupposing God's existence. It might even be considered a way that in some sense gets beneath our bedrock of knowing. We demonstrated in earlier chapters that without presupposing the validity of logic, the basic reliability of our senses, and the ability of words to communicate, we cannot know anything. We also noted that God's existence, though not our knowledge of it, precedes the existence of these three non-negotiables. We can get to the existence of God, which ontologically underpins our epistemological starting points, through what my friends call the transcendental argument for the existence of God, and what I prefer to call the epistemological argument for the existence of God.

The argument notes that none of the three nonnegotiables of knowing have a separate, independent existence. They are not eternal things, for without a knowing mind there would be no logic, without senses to perceive there would be no perception, and without two minds to communicate there would be no language. These nonnegotiables exist, we know, because they are necessary for knowing things, and we know that we know things. We know that we know things because, as we saw in our chapter on skepticism, to deny that we know things is to affirm that we know something, namely, that we cannot know things. Knowledge is inescapable, just as our own existence in inescapable. And both need a sufficient cause to explain their existence.

These nonnegotiables, we noted, are not and cannot be self-existent. Those who want to start by presupposing God make the valid point that these nonnegotiables for knowing require a source, a source that is transcendent. As we said earlier, epistemologically, we must start with how we know. We cannot skip the elements of knowing to affirm the source of those elements. But we must ask how those things by which we know came to be. The answer must be God. The argument can be reduced to this syllogism: In order for there to be knowledge, there must be a God (or a transcendent knower). There is knowledge. Therefore, there is a God. The form of the argument is valid, the classic *modus ponens* form of deduction. If the first and second premises are true, the conclusion must be true. This is the epistemological argument for the existence of God.

Paul is not saying that all those who read up on their apologetics are without excuse. He is not saying that sophisticated unbelievers need to meet up with sophisticated believers. The argument is so basic, so fundamental, that all men everywhere know it. The source of unbelief is neither a lack of information nor the failure of believers to do the work of sound apologetics. The problem is not intellectual, but moral. It is not that they cannot believe, but that they will not. And they will not believe what they already know to be true.

We are left with exactly what Paul, under the inspiration of the Holy Spirit, told us. We can either affirm the existence of the God we know, or we can be fools. This is our choice. Sophisticated intellectuals must make the same choice as ordinary people. Either they affirm the God who made them or they become the fools who say in their heart that there is no God. They either bow before their Creator or they bow before a god of their own making. Unless they repent, they will face the wrath of God that is revealed against all unrighteousness. And they will face him without any excuse that they did not know.

## CHAPTER FIFTEEN

# LOVING OUR ENEMIES

The devil began his war with God by attacking his credibility. In seducing Adam and Eve to rebel against their Maker, he succeeded in gaining two new recruits—and all who would descend from them. But God responded swiftly. His judgment upon the serpent included a powerful promise for Adam and Eve. God said, "I will put enmity between you and the woman, and between your seed and her Seed; He shall bruise your head, and you shall bruise His heel" (Gen. 3:15). Notice that God's promise is not first that he would side with us against the devil, but rather that he would cause us to side with him. He is the one who puts the enmity into the heart of the woman and into the heart of her seed. He causes us to stop fighting against him and to start fighting with him against the serpent.

It is vital as we seek to tear down strongholds, as we seek to find the lost, that we remember that in the end it is the Good Shepherd who does this. It is not our erudition that will change the hearts and minds of unbelievers.

While it is certainly true that those outside the regenerating grace of God can come to understand that God exists and that they are at war with him, as the devil himself is aware, it is also true that no man can come to love, embrace, and depend upon the truth of God unless God grants him a new heart—unless he puts enmity in the sinner's heart against the serpent. God, in short, is the one who changes hearts.

While we affirm this with vigor, however, we do not consequently cease from our calling. The fact that no amount of argumentation will ever bring someone into the kingdom of Christ does not mean that we should never argue. That God works, and his work alone can effect what we seek, in no way means that we should stop doing the work. The God who changes hearts does so through various means. Faith, we are told, comes by hearing (Rom. 10:17). This does not deny that faith is a gift from God, but affirms that God grants the gift through the hearing of the Word. In like manner, when we demonstrate the truthfulness of Christianity, we are not giving faith, but God may be using us to give grace. When Paul stood to address the crowd assembled at Mars Hill, he knew well that only God could give the increase. But he knew also that God might give the increase through his faithful proclamation and defense of the gospel. We are not being unspiritual when we seek to give an answer for the hope that is in us. We are not denying the sovereign power and authority of God. Neither are we denying the total depravity of those to whom we speak. We are merely being obedient to the call of God.

But there is much more to what we are doing. It is a great thing to defend the faith before the watching world.

It is a great thing when God uses our defense to persuade his sheep to enter into his fold. It is also a great thing when we, as his people, are instilled with greater boldness. Apologetics, rightly done, can instill courage in the hearts of God's soldiers. The bluster of the Enlightenment thinkers for too long intimidated the church into a sheepish retreat. We removed our faith from the arena of objective truth, making it subjective, experiential, and safe from attack. Wolves in academic sheepskins took on the mantle of intellectual sophistication, and we let them have it. If we bothered to affirm it at all, we affirmed that we knew that Jesus lives because he lives within our heart.

When the Enlightenment imploded and skepticism arose to replace robust optimism, the church again failed. When other truth claims failed, we failed to assert that our truth claims never failed, but were satisfied with being left alone. The heat was off. We could hold onto our private faith, which was merely "true for us," and nobody minded. We signed the peace treaty and were left without the power or the will to proclaim that what was "true" for unbelievers was objectively false.

God has put enmity between the seed of the woman and the seed of the serpent. We are engaged in a war, a war that began in Eden, that was decided at Calvary, and which will be concluded when the King returns. The King has not told us to hide in our bunkers until that time. Rather, we are called to participate in taking the land, in storming the very gates of hell. We are to do so with confidence, knowing that the gates of hell cannot prevail. We are to take every thought captive and to tear down every stronghold.

We are to do so, knowing that we are engaged in a battle of wits with half-armed enemies. We are fighting fools.

The fact that our opponents are fools ought to drive us to two other important conclusions. First, we need to remember that there, but for the grace of God, go we. We have left folly and embraced wisdom not because of our love of wisdom, but because of Wisdom's love for us. We did not enter into Christ's kingdom by the strength of our mind, but by the strength of his Spirit.

We ought to have contempt for their ideas. We cannot take the notion of a self-creating universe seriously. We should not suppress our laughter when they claim that it is objectively true that there is no objective truth. We only sully ourselves and show ourselves to be cowards and fools if we take such foolishness seriously. But we cannot forget that we once held to these ideas with all earnestness. We cannot forget that it is those who bear the image of God who believe such nonsense. And so we must respond to our foolish, hateful enemies with love.

This brings us to our second problem. We cannot let the fools define love for us. One of the reasons we have found it so easy to nap on the soft pillow of relativism is that it comes disguised as love. It is the epistemological version of "live and let live." "Live and let live" is the essence of love to the relativist. We are called to love our enemies, and we think that we should show that love by leaving them in their folly. However, this is not biblical love. It is because we love our enemies that we must laugh at their foolishness. We only encourage them in their folly when we take a nice, polite approach to their views. It is because we love those who are shooting arrows at us from their strongholds that we are called to tear them down. It is because their strongholds rest upon sinking sand that we must tear them down and, by the grace of God, lead our enemies to the Rock, so that they might no longer receive the love we owe our enemies, but the love we owe our brothers and sisters in Christ.

The spirit of relativism is gracious in that it allows us to believe almost anything. But it is a tyrant because the one view that we cannot hold is that those views that contradict our own are wrong. If there is a God, as we believe, and he has made it possible for us not only to know truth, but to know the truth that is his Word, and if that Word teaches that there is only one name under heaven by which a man can be saved, then all those who affirm that there is no God, or that he has not equipped us to know truth, or that his Word is not true, or that there are other roads to heaven, speak falsely. And the man who is that Word, who bears that name, calls us not only to say that they are false, but to show that they are false. The one true God is love, and in his love he calls us to do the work of apologetics. He calls us to answer the prophets of Baal, whatever religion or epistemology they may in our age be propagating. Because we are his, and because we believe his Word, we too show forth love. And in our love for the lost, we must be willing to accept the vilification that comes from our convictions. We are to love the lost enough to be hated for our supposed hatred of them, enough to be thought fools for proclaiming their foolishness. As we take up our arguments to take down their strongholds, we must take up our cross, and expect and accept persecution in his name.

# INDEX OF PERSONS

**R. C. Sproul Jr**. (M.A. Reformed Theological Seminary, Orlando; D.Min., Whitefield Theological Seminary) is founder of Highlands Ministries in Mendota, Virginia. He is the author and editor of several books including *When You Rise Up* and *Family Practice*.